Raising A Child With Borderline Personality Disorder: Effective Strategies To Help You Manage Your Borderline Child

CONTENTS

INTRODUCTION 1

CHAPTER 1: WHAT IS BORDERLINE PERSONALITY DISORDER?
.... 7

Psychiatric disorders, personality disorders, and bpd 8

Personality disorders 9

Where did bpd come from? the history of bpd 12

CHAPTER 2: THE SYMPTOMS AND FEATURES OF BORDERLINE PERSONALITY DISORDER 15

Emotion dysregulation 16

Unstable emotions and moods 17

Intense anger or difficulty controlling anger 18

Interpersonal dysregulation 18

Unstable and intense relationships 19

Frantic efforts to avoid abandonment 20

Behavioral dysregulation 20

Impulsivity that can be self-damaging 21

Self and identity dysregulation 22

Unstable sense of self and identity 22

Chronic feelings of emptiness 23

Cognitive dysregulation 23

Suspicious thoughts or dissociation when experiencing stress 24

How do you figure out whether you have bpd? 26

CHAPTER 3: BORDERLINE PERSONALITY DISORDER: IS WHAT THEY SAY REALLY TRUE? 28

Stigma and borderline personality disorder 29

Common myths about borderline personality disorder 30

Myth 1: people with bpd are manipulative and attention seeking 30

Myth 2: people with bpd are violent individuals and can harm others 32

Myth 3: bpd is a life sentence 34

Myth 4: bpd is untreatable 34

Myth 7: bpd is only found in women 38

CHAPTER 4: WHAT CAUSES BORDERLINE PERSONALITY DISORDER? 40

Can you inherit borderline personality disorder? 40

What about genes? 41

Personality traits, genes, and bpd 42

Borderline personality disorder and the brain 45

The limbic system and the prefrontal cortex 46

The hypothalamic-pituitary-adrenal axis (hpa) 48

Adverse life events: borderline personality disorder and the environment 49

Nature and nurture 50

Traumatic experiences and childhood maltreatment 51

Is bpd a form of post-traumatic stress disorder? 52

Invalidating environments 53

Problems with attachment 54

Factors that keep bpd going 56

Chaotic or adverse life events 56

Reinforcement: unfortunately, problematic behaviors sometimes work!
.... 57

The vicious cycle of bpd 57

CHAPTER 5: WILL I HAVE BORDERLINE PERSONALITY DISORDER FOREVER? THE COURSE OF BPD 59

The course of bpd: how long it may take to recover 60

Factors that interfere with recovery from bpd 61

Substance use disorders 62

Post-traumatic stress disorder 62

Mood and anxiety disorders 64

Other personality disorders 65

CHAPTER 6: PROBLEMS THAT OFTEN GO ALONG WITH BORDERLINE PERSONALITY DISORDER ... 67

Psychiatric disorders that often co-occur with bpd ... 67

Substance use ... 68

Escaping and avoiding emotional pain ... 68

Problems with avoiding and escaping emotional pain ... 69

Problems with using medication and substances for long periods ... 70

Eating disorders ... 70

Escaping and avoiding emotional pain ... 71

Body dissatisfaction ... 71

Sense of control ... 72

Depression ... 73

Bipolar disorder ... 75

The problem of misdiagnosis ... 75

Social anxiety disorder ... 77

Panic disorder ... 78

Post-traumatic stress disorder ... 79

CHAPTER 7: HOW DO I FIND HELP FOR MY CHILD WITH BORDERLINE PERSONALITY DISORDER? ... 81

Treading safely through the minefield: internet resources for bpd ... 82

Other ways to find information on bpd ... 85

CHAPTER 8: WHAT KINDS OF TREATMENT ARE AVAILABLE FOR CHILDREN WITH BPD? 87

Psychological treatments 88

Medications 90

What to expect when you meet with a mental health professional 90

Psychological assessments 91

Individual therapy 91

Group therapy 92

Medication treatment 93

Specific steps for getting help 93

CHAPTER 9: DEALING WITH SUICIDAL THOUGHTS 96

Steps to take if you are feeling suicidal 96

Get away from "lethal means" 97

Change the situation 99

Think about reasons to stay alive 100

Take action and challenge hopeless thinking 101

Let the thoughts come and go 102

Use any of the emotional coping skills provided in the next chapter 103

CHAPTER 10: COPING WITH YOUR EMOTIONS 104

Skills you can use to cope with emotions 104

Practice accepting your emotions and your situation right now 104

Distraction 105

Relaxation strategies 106

Progressive muscle relaxation 107

Diaphragmatic breathing 108

Slowing down your breathing 110

Mindful walking meditation 110

Better endurance: 111

Balance and coordination: 112

Increased strength: 113

Better control of your thoughts: 114

Pleasant mood: 115

Self-confidence: 115

Physical wellness: 116

Mental wellness: 117

Spiritual wellness: 117

Emotional wellness: 118

CHAPTER 11: ACTIVITIES 120

Activity 1: how can you predict the consequence of your actions?...... 120

Activity 2: learning patience 125

Activity 3: know how to follow the rules 129

Activity 4: you can have a peaceful family 134

Activity 5: you can get help when you need it 139

Conclusion 145

Resources 148

© Copyright 2021 Philip Newton M. Psych, LPC- All rights reserved.

The content contained within this book may not be reproduced, duplicated or transmitted without direct written permission from the author or the publisher.

Under no circumstances will any blame or legal responsibility be held against the publisher, or author, for any damages, reparation, or monetary loss due to the information contained within this book. Either directly or indirectly. You are responsible for your own choices, actions, and results.

Legal Notice:

This book is copyright protected. This book is only for personal use. You cannot amend, distribute, sell, use, quote or paraphrase any part, or the content within this book, without the consent of the author or publisher.

Disclaimer Notice:

Please note the information contained within this document is for educational and entertainment purposes only. All effort has been executed to present accurate, up to date, and reliable, complete information. No warranties of any kind are declared or implied. Readers acknowledge that the author is not engaging in the rendering of legal, financial, medical or professional advice. The content within this book has been derived from various sources. Please consult a licensed professional before attempting any techniques outlined in this book.

By reading this document, the reader agrees that under no circumstances is the author responsible for any losses, direct or indirect, which are incurred as a result of the use of the information contained within this document, including, but not limited to, — errors, omissions, or inaccuracies.

ABOUT THE AUTHOR

The name of the author has years of experience in managing prevalent conditions like a borderline personality disorder. Being a rehab specialist, I have all the skills and knowledge to understand your child's condition and provide you with the help you need regarding your child's uncontrolled emotions, cognitive biases, and behavioral dysregulation. Because of my extensive clinical and research-oriented expertise on the issue, I have arranged a highly practical guide for your child's BPD.

INTRODUCTION

Ellie was only thirteen years old when she cut herself. That morning started with usual activities. Ellie went to school and spent some time with her friends during recess; Rachel teased Ellie about her obesity. She told her that everyone hated her because she was so ugly and disgusting. Ellie was still pondering over the comments made by Rachel when she was coming back home. As she walked home, she became more and more agitated, scared, angry, and ashamed. Taking each step felt like losing herself, and Ellie thought she wouldn't stop feeling like this. By the time Ellie got home, she had rushed past her parents, locked herself up in her room. She was desperately trying to find a way to release all the feelings. Ellie impulsively picked up a piece of glass that was broken accidentally by her yesterday.

Children diagnosed with borderline personality disorder (BPD) constantly struggle with their emotions, behaviors and have troubles with their sense of identity. They also have difficulty in keeping healthy relationships with other people. Children with BPD often resort to coping strategies that work for a particular time. These solutions don't work most of the time, and they can worsen their problems, such as self-harming themselves to divert their attention.

Children with BPD feel that they are cruising through life at 400 MPH without breaks. They try to act swiftly in the moment rather than thinking through things. This is the reason their relationships are unstable, and they are negligent with their responsibilities. Children with BPD are emotionally sensitive; even the slightest hint of emotion can act as a trigger. Recently BPD has received enormous interest, both from the mainstream media and researchers. Researchers are busy studying the factors that are causing BPD in children and how to recover from it. They are also examining the brain areas involved in BPD and treatments that have helped people recover from BPD. There have been movies such as 'Beverly Hills' and 'Girl Interrupted', which feature characters with BPD. You may ask yourself why everyone is showing interest in BPD and why BPD is a hot topic? The better question that you should ask is; why did it take so long to get the necessary attention?

Children with BPD tend to experience intense emotional pain. They have to struggle with relentless chaos in relationships with their friends, family, and peers. They often are overwhelmed with feelings like emptiness, aloneness, and desperation.

They are confused about identifying who they are and what they are going to do in their lives. Children diagnosed with BPD have one of the highest ratios of self-harm incidents. Despite this fact, children with BPD don't have the support system that they need. BPD also influences the people near it, such as parents, friends, and caregivers. If a chemist made a potion that would create stress, concern, and heartbreak, this potion would most probably look like BPD. Treating and helping someone with BPD is like being dropped in a jet at its full speed and not knowing how to control and land it.

The high intensity of emotions and sensitivity in children with BPD can be intense and exciting. Children with BPD can also be daring and dramatic, and they are often caring and understanding. Nevertheless, caring for and helping a child with BPD is like holding a very hot and burning object. The high-intensity emotions radiating from a child with BPD can char relationships. Children with BPD often become overwhelmed by sorrow and grief, leaving the caregiver or family in the dark about the impending situation.

Many children with BPD don't know who to turn to for help, and their loved ones have no idea about the difficulties these children have to face regularly.

Although you can find practically anything on the Internet, it can be dangerous due to misinformation, and much advice are from questionable sources.

The question arises, 'How do I get useful information about BPD'? Two authentic sources that have verified information are treatment manuals and research papers. However, data from these sources can be challenging to interpret if you are not a researcher or therapist or someone relevant is not there to help you.

Parents of children with BPD must have access to up-to-date, accurate, and accessible information. They should know about the problems they are facing and how to cope up with them. That is why I wrote this book, as it will give parents and their children with BPD a road map that will guide them through the maze of their problems.

This book will be helpful if you can relate to any of the following situations:

- Your child is recently diagnosed with BPD, and you wish to learn more about the disorder.
- You want to figure out what to do with BPD.

- Your child harms himself and experiences emotional turmoil. You want your child to learn practical coping skills.
- Your child is in therapy and on medications. You still want to learn more about BPD and its causes. You want to learn how to further help your kid.
- You are a caregiver and need a comprehensive guide that tells you what to do precisely.

CHAPTER 1: WHAT IS BORDERLINE PERSONALITY DISORDER?

Rose walked through the therapist's door, and she was ready to make a change in her life. She couldn't go on to live like this forever. Although Rose was bright, intelligent, kind, and sensitive, she had been living her life like she was behind a monster truck with an enormous steering wheel, driving through the neighborhood. It seemed like she was going and destroying lawns and lampposts on her way. She looked upon the Internet about her situation and was keen to discover her problem.

I have devoted this chapter just to give you a clear picture of BPD. If you think you know someone close that might have BPD, it would be helpful to learn more about it. In this chapter, I have included the features and symptoms of BPD.
I have also added some information regarding the history of BPD.

Before starting this chapter, you must know that you cannot diagnose yourself with BPD. Although there may be some symptoms of BPD in this chapter, you may think that it's you.

You must see a professional who can give a qualified opinion on this. Trying to diagnose yourself with a psychiatric disorder is just like diagnosing yourself with cancer or heart disease.

I have met with some people who thought they had BPD, but it turned out they were suffering from depression, bipolar disorder, or PTSD. Just like heart disease and cancer have different recommended treatments, various psychiatric disorders also have different treatment methods. For an accurate diagnosis, you must see a professional who has a better understanding of the situation.

Psychiatric Disorders, Personality Disorders, and BPD

The Diagnostic and Statistical Manual of Mental Disorders is like a recipe book used by mental health professionals to list essential psychological or emotional problems. Two primary psychiatric disorders listed in this book are personality disorders and clinical disorders. According to this book, BPD is a psychiatric disorder that fits in the category of personality disorders.

Clinical Disorders

One of the psychiatric disorders is a clinical disorder or syndrome.

These disorders include depression, anxiety, panic disorders, and schizophrenia. People develop these disorders at various points in their lives. Some of these disorders last for a short period, such as panic disorder, while some may last for very long periods like schizophrenia.

Personality Disorders

The other type is a personality disorder. The most asked question is 'what is a personality disorder?' We all have typical ways of acting, which includes our personality. A personality disorder, simply put, is a long-lasting pattern and practice of acting to the actions around us that don't work very well. This causes problems and puts obstacles in the way of reaching goals in life. Many personality disorders include obsessive-compulsive, histrionic, narcissistic, antisocial, paranoid, and of course, borderline personality disorder.

Having a set of problems with you for an extended period usually is a personality disorder. Many people diagnosed with BPD have had issues since their childhood. Having a personality disorder doesn't mean that you have a flawed personality or possess a bad character.

It doesn't in any sense make you an unlikeable person; you need to get these myths out of your head.

The central assumption about BPD is that a person has something in their personality that tends to make some problems for them and other people around them. Nevertheless, we don't agree with this for a few reasons. For example, phrases like 'bad character' or 'problematic person' are often used instead of complex personality, and as understood before, using it in this way is not accurate. Secondly, this term suggests that the problem is inside you; basically, you are the problem. We disagree with this point of view. Much evidence and scientific research shows that environmental factors such as trauma, abuse, and other factors like stress play a pivotal role in psychological problems, including personality disorders. Also, placing the issue inside you creates stigma and judgemental reactions on other people. The term 'personality disorder' suggests that you always had this problem, and you will always have it.

However, as you will see in this book, there is evidence that BPD doesn't last as long as people think it does. So having BPD doesn't mean that you will always have problems in your personality and that you will always struggle with it. It simply means that your thinking pattern hinders your ability to live a quality life and reach your goals.

The matter is complicated because the book I mentioned above treats psychiatric disorders and uses the 'disease model' for psychological disorders. The book mentioned above relates psychiatric disorders with some kind of pathology in the individual or in an environment, much like diseases like flu, diabetes, etc.

The main problem with this idea is that psychiatric disorders tend to operate differently compared with diseases. The first fact is that you can't catch a psychiatric disorder like a disease such as flu. Secondly, like a disease, psychiatric disorders are not linked with any physical malfunction.

The third fact is that many of the symptoms found in one disorder are also present in another, making the line between different psychiatric disorders blurry, unlike in a disease with a particular set of symptoms for one condition.

Fourth, diagnoses for disorders are based on what you think, feel, or do, while specific tests determine the underlying disease in a disease. Fifth, a disease model places the problem inside of you. In BPD, many problems you struggle with are in an environment rather than problems inside you. Therefore, I believe that what you do, think, and feel is more essential than whether you have some disorder or not.

Where Did BPD Come From? The History of BPD

It is essential to know something about the history of BPD. In the 19th century, people used borderline to describe the fuzzy border of two psychiatric disorders.

It was a common perception that there were two large categories of psychiatric disorders. One was called 'neurosis', which involved patients that knew about the reality but had emotional problems, such as depression or panic disorders.

The other category was psychosis, which involved patients who experienced hallucinations not based on reality, such as schizophrenia. The psychiatrists put patients in the borderline category who didn't have serious problems labeled as psychotic but were much troubled to be called 'neurotic'. The term "borderline" was used for patients who had trouble seeing the good and bad at the same time.

Many ways of thinking about BPD at that time came from observing the limited number of patients, and the study was not based on scientific research but only on myths and common assumptions at that time.

Since the early days, many kinds of research have been conducted. Many findings of the critical characteristic now make up borderline personality disorder, which includes the varying intensity of emotions, impulsive behavior, identity, and relationship problems. Those who are diagnosed with BPD are no longer identified on the spectrum of psychosis and neurosis. Science is helping us keep up with the new ideas of BPD and is helping to discard old beliefs that are inaccurate.

SPECIAL BONUS!

Want this bonus book for free?

Get FREE unlimited access to it and all of my new books by joining the Fan Base!

  SCAN W/YOUR CAMERA TO JOIN!

CHAPTER 2: THE SYMPTOMS AND FEATURES OF BORDERLINE PERSONALITY DISORDER

Carl, for a long time, knew that there was something different about him. Since childhood, he has been very emotional about little things. It seemed like Carl had always been crying or getting excited about the things that were not worth it. Although Carl possesses a great deal of empathy for others, his struggle with intense emotions has caused various problems. It led to conflict in his relationships, making it hard for Carl to focus on one task or job.

BPD, simply put, is a disorder of unstable emotions. Children with BPD are inconsistent in their feelings. They have difficulty identifying themselves and struggle to maintain relationships. Children with BPD are often afraid of being abandoned. Emotionally they feel like they are on a roller coaster ride: out of their control and emotions going up and down in a jiff. They also have a sudden outburst of anger. Children with BPD also act impulsively when they feel overwhelmed and often resort to self-harm when they're upset. BPD children have trouble thinking clearly.

Dr Marsha Linehan, who developed an effective treatment plan for BPD, put nine symptoms in five different understandable categories.

1. Emotional dysregulation.
2. Interpersonal dysregulation.
3. Behavioral dysregulation.
4. Cognitive dysregulation.
5. Identity of self-dysregulation.

Notice that the term dysregulation pops in all five categories. Dysregulated means 'not controlled.' Indeed, children with BPD are unstable and have difficulty controlling their lives. Next, we will expand these categories and elaborate on the different features that fall within them.

Emotion Dysregulation

As a child, Carl was very emotional and struggled with managing his emotions. He remembered walking towards his class on his very first day in kindergarten, terrified of other students there and frozen in one place. As a grown kid, Carl still feels agitated and irritated at minor inconveniences, such as the sound of nails scratching and the sound of a chalkboard.

Despite trying his best, he still cannot control his anger. Carl still has random and sudden anger outbursts, which have led to problems with other students around him in the classroom. He is constantly feeling ashamed, guilty, and empty.

Emotional dysregulation means having unstable emotions and difficulty in managing emotions effectively. According to some researchers, emotional dysregulation is the most critical problem for children with BPD. Many of the issues are mostly tracked back to emotional dysregulation. Unstable emotions and difficulty in controlling emotions and anger fall under the category of emotional dysregulation.

Unstable Emotions and Moods

Children with BPD often react to things that would not affect other people. For instance, if you have BPD, you might notice that you quickly get upset by what others do or say. You promptly get stressed out at little things more rapidly than other people. Minor criticism or a concerned look make you stressed, and your get in emotional turmoil. This makes people with BPD to be happy one minute and sad at the very next moment.

Intense Anger or Difficulty Controlling Anger

Having intense anger or struggling to control it is just another feature of BPD. Children with BPD are easily irritated and angered at things that might not upset other people. They are unable to control themselves in this scenario and start yelling and throwing things. Although anger is one criterion for BPD, BPD children are also easily overwhelmed by feelings of shame, sadness, and guilt. Some kids with BPD tend to be more upset at themselves instead of anyone else.

Interpersonal Dysregulation

Although Carl was charming and soulful, he often felt like he was on a roller-coaster ride in his relationship with friends and family members. A slight criticism or a disapproving look felt like a knife piercing through his gut.

Interpersonal dysregulation means struggling to have meaningful relationships with people around you. It definitely doesn't mean that you are a terrible or unlikeable person. In fact, children with BPD are pretty charming, engaging, and enjoyable. Nevertheless, they struggle in their relationships in two ways:

1. They have unstable and rocky relationships.
2. They have a fear of abandonment.

Unstable and Intense Relationships

Kids with BPD have rocky relations with their peers and friends. Their intense emotions sometimes become challenging for their friends. If you have BPD, you may have noticed that sometimes things go unbelievably well for you in your social life, and it starts to fall apart in other instances. Like emotions, relationships also feel like a roller-coaster ride, and you seem to have no control over them.

Diagnostic and Statistical Manual of Mental Disorders (DSM-IV-TR) Criteria for Borderline Personality Disorder include:

- Desperate efforts to avoid being abandoned in reality or in imagination.
- A pattern of intense and unstable personal relationships, which often alternates between extremes of devaluation and idealization.
- Have trouble identifying themselves.
- Unstable sense of relief and self-image.
- Impulsive in two areas that are potentially self-harming.

- Show suicidal behavior, or threats, or self-harming behavior.
- Chronic feelings of emptiness.
- Intense anger or difficulty in managing anger.
- Stress-related ideation and severe dissociative symptoms.

Frantic Efforts to Avoid Abandonment

Another feature present in children with BPD is fear of being abandoned. In fact, some researchers believe that fear of being abandoned is the most crucial cause of the problems in children with BPD. These children often feel panic outbursts whenever a relationship with their friend, therapist, partner, or family member ends. They think that they will be alone and that there will be no one to support them in such a critical situation. This feeling of being alone or left unattended can be so intense that they can go to great lengths to convince that person not to leave them. They beg and plead and even try to start a fight or physically stop that person from leaving.

Behavioral Dysregulation

Carl was a straight-A student in his class, and he was consistently good in his academics. Just before his graduation, he dropped out of his course.

He replied, 'I just couldn't handle the pressure when asked why he dropped out. When Carl was upset, he would react to the situation impulsively without thinking it through.

He would often lock himself up in his room and start to scratch himself so that the pain could distract him from his miseries.

Behavioral dysregulation means that the child's behavior is out of control, negatively affecting the child's life. There are signs that your child can harm themselves and your child often struggles in two primary ways: risky impulsivity and self-harm.

Impulsivity That Can Be Self-Damaging

Children with BPD tend to harm themselves. For instance, your child may do things recklessly, play dangerous sports, or binge on food. Your child may know that these behaviors are not suitable for them, but they still do it regardless of the consequences.

In my experience, children with BPD react impulsively and recklessly because they are upset, and to get relief from the pain, they engage in such activities.

Self and Identity Dysregulation

Carl was always making drastic changes in his life and was always unsure what he wanted to do after finishing his schooling.

One day he wanted to be a scientist, and another day he wanted to be an astronaut. Another day Carl decided that he hated being an astronaut, so he wanted to pursue a career in geography. At one point, he even wanted to change his religion. In a session with his therapist, he said that he has no idea what he really wants and has an identity crisis; he often feels completely different.

With self and identity dysregulation, a person does not have a clear or stable sense of who they are and can also feel empty much of the time.

Unstable Sense of Self and Identity

Children diagnosed with BPD often struggle with their sense of identity. If you have BPD, you may notice that your sense of yourself is entirely changing, depending on the situation. You may act and feel different in different situations. Children with BPD don't have a clear sense of who they are and where life is taking them.

The disturbing part of an identity crisis is not having a sense of your core identity.

Chronic Feelings of Emptiness

Another part of identity or self-dysregulation is feeling empty inside all of the time. Some children with BPD reported that they felt a void inside them. They think they are missing something essential. This feeling is very uncomfortable and awkward for them to describe and lasts for long periods.

Cognitive Dysregulation

Another problem Carl frequently reported was that he struggled with being spaced out, and negative thoughts always clouded his mind. When Carl was upset, he did some things that he would forget about later. Sometimes he feels that he cannot trust anyone near him, and other people around him try to harm him or take advantage of him.

Cognitive dysregulation causes a person to think negatively and feel disconnected from their surrounding environment. You must know that your child is going through stress or is really upset when exhibiting this behavior.

Suspicious Thoughts or Dissociation When Experiencing Stress

Another problem in this area is paranoid thinking. BPD children are always thinking about others' motives. If you are also struggling with this, it doesn't mean that you are delusional or psychotic.

It means when you are upset, you start to worry about how others feel about you. You may start thinking that people are trying to take advantage of you or they are trying to harm you. You may feel this when you are under a lot of stress, and you are really upset. You will not experience it when everything is normal.

Another aspect of cognitive dysregulation is dissociation. This may make you feel spaced out and think that you are not inside your body. Some children reported they felt as if they were floating on the ceiling.

Not Everyone with BPD Is alike

You may have noticed that out of nine ingredients for BPD, you have to fall on a minimum of five symptoms. You might be thinking that there can be hundreds of different combinations for these nine symptoms, and falling on them would be called BPD?

You can be correct as there are 151 different ways to meet the criteria, which means that everyone's disorder is not similar.

Imagine a diagnosis called 'businessperson.' When you think of it, you may think they:

1. Wear fancy suits.
2. Have an expensive office.
3. Always think about money.
4. Meet rich people.
5. Sell things.
6. Work long hours.
7. Do lots and lots of paperwork.
8. They are highly successful.
9. Get up early for work.

It takes only five of the features to be labelled as a 'businessperson.' This means that two businesspeople may be entirely different. Sam, for instance, doesn't work as much, wears shorts, gets up late, does no paperwork, but is still highly successful and earns loads of money.

Jack, in contrast, always gets up early, works long hours, does lots of paperwork, and wears expensive suits, but is still unsuccessful and has failed in many businesses.

Think of being diagnosed with BPD in a similar way. Two people with BPD rarely show a similar pattern of behavior.

How Do You Figure Out Whether You Have BPD?

As we have discussed earlier, the best way to determine if your child has BPD is to consult a qualified professional to make a diagnosis. It is recommended that you seek a professional with extensive training and experience with personality disorders and get an assessment. An accurate diagnosis is vital, and this may require lots of talking on behalf of a patient. A professional will help you in distinguishing between BPD and other disorders like bipolar disorder or depression.

CHAPTER 3: BORDERLINE PERSONALITY DISORDER: IS WHAT THEY SAY REALLY TRUE?

All health professionals, clinicians, and researchers agree that access to information is crucial to the recovery process, regardless of the problems you are struggling to cope with. For psychiatric disorders, having accurate information is essential. For instance, if you are visiting a friend in California without having his address and street number, it would make your trip very confusing, stressful, and overwhelming; the same is the case with BPD.

Having specific information gives you a clear sense of what is going on with your body, mind, and your life in general. Simply knowing the facts about your disorder is one of the vital steps in recovering from the condition.

Although accurate information is readily available, unfortunately, we are still surrounded by lots of misinformation. This makes it difficult to separate what is authentic from what is just fiction. This phenomenon makes a recovery much more difficult.

Despite all of the new discoveries about BPD, we are still surrounded by persistent myths that lead people in the wrong way and add more stigma. In this part, we will take a look at common myths and misconceptions about BPD.

Stigma and Borderline Personality Disorder

Although all mental disorders have a social stigma attached to them, the stigma with BPD is powerful. Many organizations, such as NAMI, have worked tirelessly to reduce the social stigma attached to BPD. Nowadays, we see fewer negative portrayals of BPD due to awareness, but the stigma associated with BPD is still persistent in society.

There are few reasons why society stigmatizes people with BPD. The first reason is the cause of BPD is poorly understood, and some people react negatively to problems that they don't understand. Sadly, symptoms of BPD hit the nerve of some people in our society. They are unable to relate to people with BPD and cannot understand their behavior of self-harm which scares them off.

Another source of stigma is television and media. The media seems to be drawn towards BPD, probably because of some of the strengths of BPD. These strengths can be an exciting, charismatic, and dramatic personality.

The media and TV always try to depict the substantial aspects of BPD and frequently blow them out of proportionality. Showing only the excellent side contributes to the stigma attached to BPD and makes it harder for the public to understand the genuine concept.

Common Myths About Borderline Personality Disorder

There are continued myths and negative portrayals of BPD in mainstream media. We must clear up common and problematic myths. Below I have compiled a list of the most common myths that surround BPD.

Myth 1: People with BPD Are Manipulative and Attention Seeking

This is one of the common myths about BPD. It is so common that it is also found in research literature and clinical academic papers in addition to mainstream media. This myth developed as a misguided try to explain the self-harm aspect of BPD.

A self-harm action can trigger emotional responses such as guilt, sadness, fear, and confusion. Many people in this situation jump to help the person who is engaging in self-harming behavior.

It is a common desire to help the person with serious problems, but ironically, people believe that people with BPD are manipulative.

Some health professionals in the past may have concluded that a person involved in self-harming situations is just doing it so that others can pay attention to them and help them. The problem here is that you cannot deduce someone's intentions from their behavior.

Let's say that you are in a hurry to get to work as you are late; on your way, you were careless about the red light and hit a pedestrian. Saying that a person with BPD harms themselves to get support is like saying you skipped a red light to hit the pedestrian. We may not know the real scenario, and if we assume something about it, we can go towards a wrong conclusion. The same principle applies here. We cannot believe that another person is engaging in self-harm behavior to get our attention. Influencing others through their behavior is not the primary reason people with BPD hurt themselves.

Even if the person with BPD learned that the only way to get attention is through self-harm, their behavior does not mean they are manipulative.

This simply means that they have not yet learned how to ask for help or attentiveness from another person, and this is the only way they know they will get it. Getting attention from other humans is a basic need of a person. We would want to get positive attention from everyone around us rather than negative.

In BPD cases, people are ready to have negative attention due to lack of engagement. So, the assumption of being manipulative means overlooking a basic human need.

The message I am trying to communicate is people with BPD are not manipulative. This behavior serves an essential purpose for them that an outside observer cannot readily see.

Myth 2: People with BPD Are Violent Individuals and can harm others

This perception is absolutely wrong. Despite the way people with BPD are portrayed on media, they are not generally violent and are actually at low risk of hurting others.

In many cases, children with BPD simply try to avoid hurting others and go out of their way to sacrifice their needs to make others happy. They wouldn't want to do anything that may cause others to leave or reject them.

Most researchers have concluded that children with BPD are far more likely to hurt themselves rather than a person near them. A child with BPD exhibits self-harming behavior, and the anger they show is inward rather than outward. It is essential to note that children with BPD are terrified of showing anger and avoiding experiencing or expressing anger.

In some cases, it is due to their history of childhood abuse and trauma, including emotional and physical abuse. After experiencing abuse for many years, some people with BPD have zero tolerance towards it and vow never to abuse anyone intentionally.

Myth 3: BPD Is a Life Sentence

People thought that BPD was incurable in the past, and once you had this, there was no going back. You were stuck with it forever. This was the primary reason clinicians refused to treat children with BPD. We now know that this is not valid, and there is an excellent prognosis for BPD.

In fact, recent research shows a higher chance of recovery from BPD than bipolar disorder. All of this is due to the increased public awareness about the BPD.

The most important thing to take away is that BPD is curable, and many people have recovered and gone on to live the life they always wanted.

Myth 4: BPD Is Untreatable

This myth is related to previous myths, and it is an interesting one due to the way it developed. Many health professionals in the past had difficulty in treating BPD, and there were often struck with zero improvements from the patient. They concluded that BPD was not treatable.

This is similar to going to the gym and lifting 100 kg's of weight, and after being unable to lift the weight, you conclude that lifting 100 kg's is impossible. The same was the case with BPD. Without any specialized study and understanding of BPD, it was supposed that BPD was untreatable. The fact that the early treatments didn't work doesn't mean that BPD cannot be treated. Fortunately, advances in science and scientific research on the topic have helped us to learn more about it and have removed any myths that came with BPD.

Myth 5: BPD Is Caused by Bad Parents

Many health professionals thought that BPD was caused by the stormy relationship of the patients with their parents in the early part of childhood.

Mothers were frequently blamed if their child was diagnosed with any psychiatric disorders. 'Bad mothering' was the term used when a child was diagnosed with the condition. Although this misconception has mainly been removed, it is still believed that mental disorders are caused by bad parenting in some societies.

There are a couple of things that must be kept in mind. First, there is a difference between the increased risk of disorders and the necessary cause of the condition. Abuse contributes to increasing the risk of disorder but doesn't cause the disorder.
In fact, in many cases, patients didn't have any history of abuse. The same thing applies to neglect.

The takeaway is, some facts cause the disorder to increase while others can cure the condition, and you must know that terrible parenting increases risk rather than causing the disorder.

Myth 6: People with BPD Are Crazy and Irrational
This myth cannot be further from the truth. Children diagnosed with BPD are in intense pain and are struggling with intense, overwhelming emotions all the time. Sometimes, these struggles get the better of them, which leads them to say or do somewhat inappropriate things.

Although they regret this later, these actions provide them relief from intense emotional pain at the moment.

We know that behaviors have a particular purpose and meet the critical need of the individual exhibiting the behavior. Although these behaviors are not irrational or crazy, it gives them a sense of relief for some time.

The problem is that these behaviors coupled with self-destructive activities have severe downsides for them in the long run.

It is essential to take note that people with BPD are not inherently different from other people. They are not aliens or made up of some other substances. In fact, they have the same personality traits that we all have. One of the personality traits of people with BPD is 'neuroticism,' which means negative emotions. We all experience negative emotions, but people with BPD tend to experience these emotions for longer periods and with higher intensity.

Although some of the behavior of BPD children may seem irrational, they are pretty reasonable and understandable through a thought process.

Children with BPD constantly fear that everyone will abandon them, and fear of being left alone is always persistent in them. This is because, in many cases, children with BPD have faced actual abandonment and rejection. As a result, it is natural that they might expect this behavior from other people.

Myth 7: BPD Is Only Found in Women

At a basic level, this myth is wrong. BPD can also be found in men. In fact, research shows that men with BPD have the same problems and struggle with the same situations as women do, and this disorder looks the same in both genders. Nevertheless, we know that men can also be diagnosed with BPD, but statistically, it is found more in women than men (about three times more). I really don't know the primary reason why the ratio of women diagnosed is more than men, but I have some reasons that can shed some light on it.

One possible explanation is the way boys and girls are raised. Because children are taught that expressing emotions, being emotional, and relying on relationships are common characteristics of women, this may cause boys to express their feelings in different ways when in distress. For instance, rather than crying, males tend to behave aggressively.

Another reason is that clinicians are most likely to diagnose women with BPD simply because of gender stereotypes. As clinicians may have noticed that BPD is more persistent in women than men, they may not see it in men. Similarly, BPD also has features that are more acceptable in women than in men.

This may lead clinicians to believe that this disorder is restricted to women and may overlook men's cases.

CHAPTER 4: WHAT CAUSES BORDERLINE PERSONALITY DISORDER?

In this part, we will go through the causes of BPD. You must keep in mind that no one is 100% sure what causes BPD. But many studies show that BPD is the combination of genetics, biological reactions, personality traits, and stressful experiences.

Can You Inherit Borderline Personality Disorder?

Ben's family was always a little different from others. They reacted strangely to small things and became very upset and stressed about minor issues. His family argued most of the time. Ben often saw scars or cuts on his mother's arms. He knew that he and his family had the same problems when he went for therapy.

One frequently asked question is, can the BPD be inherited from parents? To answer the question through proper evidence, researchers took a set of identical twins, and as they shared the same ovum, they shared 100% genes.

The set of fraternal twins came from different ova and shared 50% of their genes.

Only a few cases were studied, and it was found through the cases that, if you have BPD, the chance of your identical twin having BPD is 35%. At the same time, the fraternal twin has a chance of 7% of having BPD. These researches suggest that BPD is partially inherited, and some indicate that BPD may be about 50% inheritable.

Studies have found a 10-20 percent chance that a first-degree relative will have BPD if you have BPD. This is relatively low, but you still have to factor in the 1.6 percent chance of the prevalence rate of BPD. This puts you at risk of getting BPD if your relative has already been diagnosed with BPD, which is 12 times higher than the general population.

What About Genes?

If we assume that BPD is heritable, then the question that arises is 'what kind of genes cause BPD?' There is no clear answer to this question. Simply stated, your genes influence the environment, and ultimately, the environment will influence your genes' activity.

To conclude, genes don't cause BPD independently, but a specific set of genes in a particular environment can cause BPD.

To our knowledge, there is no published study that can relate specific genes to BPD. The best we can do is look at the research on genes involved in traits that go along with BPD.

Personality Traits, Genes, and BPD

Ben was always an impulsive and emotional person. Many people liked him for these traits. He was very popular in his school, and he was willing to take risks that others wouldn't dare take. Due to his impulsive behavior, he would get into activities that were bad for his health. He was also a compassionate person and would be hurt at little criticism. He felt all the emotions at high intensity, whether they were sad, happy, or anxious.

As BPD is a personality disorder, you might be wondering what kinds of traits are related to BPD. Personality traits are the way a particular person thinks, acts, and feels. When someone says you are very social and extroverted, they are talking about your personality traits.

One trait of BPD is impulsiveness, which tends to be acting quickly or spurring the moment—making a rash decision without thinking about the consequences. The impulsive feature of BPD can get you in trouble and cause you lots of distress.

Indeed, children with BPD are more impulsive than children diagnosed with other disorders. BPD children also have different personality traits that are similar to impulsivity. Studies showed that people with gene DRD4 have lower dopamine levels, which increases the intensity of impulsivity in the human body. Although this gene doesn't explain all impulsive behavior, the findings have been mixed so far. Future studies of gene DRD4 may help us better understand the connection between dopamine and impulsivity in children with BPD.

When serotonin genes are low, they cause negative emotions, which forms another set of personality traits related to children with BPD. One of the traits is neuroticism which increases one's intensity to experience negative emotions. So if you have BPD, you have probably experienced loads of negative emotions. We all experience negative emotions, but children with BPD experience these emotions with high intensity, which tend to last longer in these children.

It is not surprising that children with BPD face these rollercoasters of emotions. There is nothing wrong with experiencing negative emotions; what your child does after experiencing these emotions is essential.

Some researchers believe that brain chemical serotonin might be related to negative emotions, which further causes depression, anxiety, and neuroticism. Studies have shown that children who have a high rate of neuroticism have a specific gene related to low serotonin levels. So, having low serotonin levels and a high rate of neuroticism may put you at a higher risk of developing BPD.

Borderline Personality Disorder and the Brain

Ben told his therapist," There is always something weird about me. I am not like other people, and I don't react to situations like them." He described how he felt that his brain and thoughts were spinning out of control. He couldn't think clearly and was struggling to calm himself down. He always wondered if his brain was different from other people's brains or whether he was just crazy.

You may have noticed that you react to things differently as compared to other people. You think differently, and you feel intense emotions.

You have trouble stopping yourself from acting impulsively. If so, you may have wondered that your brain might be different from other people.

It is not as simple as it seems because the brain is a very complex organ of the body with different structures and systems that interact with each other. Many factors influence the growth of the brain. Children with BPD could have differences in their brains due to genes or exposure to unhealthy substances and conditions. Stressful events during infancy and impoverished conditions can affect the brain in several ways.

Below, we will go through the areas of the brain that may be involved in BPD.

The Limbic System and the Prefrontal Cortex

This part of your brain has to deal with emotions, memory, and pleasure. Some of the structure in the limbic system includes amygdala and hippocampus. Amygdala is the emotional center of the brain. When you get emotional or experience something, the sensitive amygdala gets active. In contrast, the hippocampus is the learning and memory center of the brain.

It is not surprising that researchers have found differences in the amygdala in children with BPD compared with children who don't have BPD. Research shows that children with BPD have a smaller amygdala, and specific areas of their amygdala are more reactive to sensitive situations. Children with BPD have strong activity in their left amygdalas.

Research has also revealed that children with BPD tend to have a smaller hippocampus than children who don't have BPD. Another interesting thing to note is that people diagnosed with PTSD also have a smaller hippocampus, but among people with BPD, both amygdala and hippocampus are smaller.

Another area of the brain that seems to be involved in BPD is the prefrontal cortex. It is a small but very complex area of the brain. It is an important part that helps us control our behavior, make reasoned decisions, and help us deal with our emotions.

There is evidence that the prefrontal cortex influences the activity in the limbic system. It keeps the activity of emotions in the amygdala in check. If children with BPD have a low level of activity in the prefrontal cortex, amygdala activity is not scrutinized.

As a result, in a stressful event, emotions spin out of control.

The Hypothalamic-Pituitary-Adrenal Axis (HPA)

HPA axis is another area of the brain that is related to BPD. Two structures within the HPA are the hypothalamus and pituitary gland. Both these parts influence the body's response to stress. Higher activity in HPA correlates with the higher concentration of stress hormones called cortisol. The more active the HPA axis is the more cortisol that will be found in your system. An overly enthusiastic HPA axis means that you have a hyperactive stress response.

If your child has BPD, you may have noticed that minor stressors to other children throw your kid over the edge. Your child gets easily irritated and frustrated over small things if they don't go their way.

Some research on the BPA axis has shown that children with BPD have exaggerated cortisol responses compared to those who don't have BPD. Other studies revealed that hyperactivity in the HPA axis might predispose people to do actions related to self-harm. Traumatic life events can also cause to have an exaggerated cortisol response in the HPA axis.

It makes sense because when you are really hurt or severely traumatized, your body might decide to prepare your system just in case it happens again. The cortisol response is your body responding to the stress.

Your body may start to become too reactive if you are experiencing stress consistently. You may be stressed out even after relatively minor things. This happens to all of us, but its intensity is higher in children with BPD and happens more often. This might be partly due to the traumatic events you have faced in the past.

Adverse Life Events: Borderline Personality Disorder and the Environment

Ben was unable to take control of his life. It felt like he was always in the middle of trouble. Although he was not abused as a child, his parents ignored him while growing up, and his parents got angry at him whenever he was upset. When his uncle died, Ben couldn't stop crying. At first, his parents were nice to him and consoled him, but later told him to get over it. At one point, they yelled at him to stop crying.

As discussed earlier, BPD is a complex disorder, and its causes are also as complex as the disorder. Many things have to come together for someone to have BPD.

Specific life experiences may also cause BPD. BPD is not just about how you were born but also how you grew through your life experiences.

Nature and Nurture

You may have heard 'nature vs. nurture' which states whether psychiatric disorders are due to the genetic factors you are born with (nature) or the factors related to the environment you grow up in (nurture). However, this debate is outdated; scientific research suggests that both genetics and environment play an essential role in psychiatric disorders.

Traumatic Experiences and Childhood Maltreatment

The environmental factor in BPD that is frequently discussed is childhood maltreatment. It is precisely what it sounds like, mistreatment, being neglected, or being abused. Many studies have indicated a link between childhood abuse and BPD. Although the findings vary in studies, about half of the people with BPD were abused sexually as a child. Cognitive symptoms of BPD include dissociation. Dissociation is common among people who have undergone trauma.

It can become a problem for those experiencing it as they find relief in dissociation, and it can become an addiction for them to dissociate from society.

Another cognitive symptom of BPD is suspiciousness. It makes the child not trust others and negatively think of everything. If someone in your childhood abused you, you would find it difficult to trust anyone, and you will have suspicious thoughts from time to time. Being abused in childhood makes it difficult to feel secure in any relationship, primarily if the abuser was closely related.

Overall, there is evidence present that abuse is somewhat connected with the problems that are typical of BPD. However, abuse alone cannot cause BPD, but it increases the risk associated with BPD.

Is BPD a Form of Post-traumatic stress disorder?

Because of BPD and abuse, many people think that BPD is an advanced form of post-traumatic stress disorder (PTSD). PTSD is a disorder that develops after experiencing frightening, horrifying, or traumatic events.

In PTSD, you experience traumatic events again, especially when you are sleeping. You even have flashbacks of the trauma while doing the routine work. Abuse is one type that may cause PTSD.

After careful consideration, I and some other experts have concluded that BPD is not a form of PTSD. This is the fact for a couple of reasons. First, almost 50% of children with BPD have not reported childhood abuse, and up to 54% don't even meet the criteria for PTSD. Second, some children with BPD haven't experienced a traumatic event in the past. To be diagnosed with PTSD, you have to experience an extremely traumatic event. Although BPD and PTSD sometimes go hand in hand, not everyone with BPD has PTSD. We can conclude that PTSD is a separate psychiatric disorder, although trauma does play a significant role in BPD for some children.

Invalidating Environments

Other than abuse, growing up in an invalidating environment can also lead to BPD. An invalidating environment is one in which people think that their thoughts and feelings are not valid, genuine, reasonable, or understandable. In this environment, your child can be punished, ignored, or criticized.

Growing up in invalidating environment leads to many problems that are common among children with BPD. For instance, if your parents got angry at you or punished you after you got upset, you might become afraid of your feelings and emotions.

You may think that there is something wrong with you because of these worrying emotions that you feel. You shouldn't be so upset. Indeed, children diagnosed with BPD often struggle with trusting themselves with their feelings, chastising themselves for being so sensitive.

Invalidating environments can also make some children with BPD spin out of control, as the climate is not responding back consistently in the way they are expecting. Some researchers have shown that people prefer it if they get feedback from others and it matches the way they feel about themselves. As discussed earlier, difficulty in managing one's emotions is not a BPD person's strongest suit. An invalidating environment doesn't help in managing one's emotions.

Problems with Attachment

Another environmental factor that increases the problem is the emotional bond with other people.

Many health professionals believe that healthy relationships with people around you are suitable for mental health and fulfilling relationships.

Some children with BPD may not have healthy, steady, and fulfilling relationships. One study found out that children with BPD often described their parents as overcontrolling and indifferent. This type of influence creates an invalidating environment that we have discussed previously.

Lousy parenting leads to a disorganized attachment style. Children with disorganized attachment styles show conflicting responses, sometimes they seek closeness with their mother, and sometimes they resist a simple touch from their mother.

One of the tendencies of BPD is to go back and forth in your thinking about other people. The disorganized attachment style further paves the way for BPD behavior as they consistently have trouble trusting people around them.

Factors That Keep BPD Going

It is also essential to know about the factors that maintain the BPD over time.

After careful research, I have listed below a couple of factors that might maintain the problems related to BPD.

Chaotic or Adverse Life Events

One of the factors may be adverse or chaotic life events. In my experience, children with BPD experience loads of unpleasant and stressful affairs. You might have noticed that crises and stressful events keep coming into your life.

Conflict with other people around you is the most common stressor and is a common trigger among children with BPD. While being rejected, left alone, humiliated, or failing at something is also expected to trigger self-harming intentions among children with BPD.

Being exposed to a chaotic lifestyle keeps the problems going with you. If you are frequently under stress, you may get frustrated quickly, and you become emotionally vulnerable.

Reinforcement: Unfortunately, Problematic Behaviors Sometimes Work!

Another factor that helps in BPD is that some behaviors that go with BPD work pretty well in the short term. Some impulsive behaviors provide relief for a short period.

As they are whimsical, children with BPD continue to engage in these activities even though they are harmful to them in the long term. They still do this because it provides them with a temporary solution.

It is challenging to eliminate these activities from a child's life. According to these children, it provides them with the relief and solution they are always looking for.

The Vicious Cycle of BPD

It is sad to imagine that this kind of reinforcement gets you in a vicious cycle. First, you feel an extremely stressful event (for instance, someone humiliates you), then you feel emotionally distressed (sad, ashamed, and angry).

If your child is diagnosed with BPD, you will probably have a hard time making your child feel better. You have to be cautious because, at this stage, your child may involve himself in such activity that may provide him with some relief for the short term but will destroy his life in the long run. These activities will lead to more problems in the future. Your child is likely to engage in the same issues that have helped your child in the past.

CHAPTER 5: WILL I HAVE BORDERLINE PERSONALITY DISORDER FOREVER? THE COURSE OF BPD

When Emma was in hospital after she harmed herself, her psychiatrist told her about her BPD. She was relieved to hear this because she now knew about the root cause of her problems. After a couple of months, she started to get worried again as she wanted to learn more about BPD. How will she deal with it in the future?

When diagnosed with a psychiatric disorder, you must know what to expect as the condition progresses. It is pretty scary to be diagnosed with a psychological illness. There is not a lot of information available on how long BDP lasts.

Simply knowing what to expect as the disorder progresses and what is likely to happen as you or your child grow with BPD eliminates the unpredictability and uncertainty, making the condition less scary and manageable. This helps in planning ahead and prepares you to cope better with the disorder.

In the past, people thought that BPD lasted forever, and it was one of the few reasons why it was called 'personality disorder.' However, we now know that disorders are not stable. In fact, it is safe to assume that BPD will change over time or even go away. Some people still believe that it is a myth to recover from BPD. This is why you must read this section for accurate information to recover from BPD.

One important thing to consider is that symptoms of BPD vary in their intensity over time. Some symptoms get better or worse, and some go away or stick with you for a long time. Knowing about the symptom and their variations will help you understand what to expect in the recovery process.

The Course of BPD: How Long It May Take to Recover

Mental health professionals once thought that BPD was a lifelong disorder; their assessment was solely based on ill-founded assumptions and anecdotal evidence. In fact, up until very recently, there was no scientific research that could tell how long BPD would last. However, time is changing, and more research is being done about the recovery process. There is a lot of evidence that points out that most of the people diagnosed with BPD will no longer fall on the disorder's criteria after six years.

Research revealed that 74 percent of the patients diagnosed with BPD no longer met the requirements of BPD after six years. Ninety-four percent of them never met the same criteria again over their lifetime. For many people, BPD went and stayed away instead of flaring back.

When diagnosed with BPD, there is more hope for the children and adults to recover than other psychiatric disorders such as bipolar or depression. These disorders tend to come back again during the patient's life.

It is worth noticing that the six-year recovery rate is not 100 percent. This is because some children make a slow recovery, and there may be some obstacles in the path of the recovery process. For instance, it is harder for you or your child to recover from BPD if coupled with another disorder.

Factors That Interfere with Recovery from BPD

This section boils down to the fact that recovery from BPD is slower and challenging if they have another psychological disorder along with BPD. Some of the disorders that make it harder to recover are listed below:

Substance Use Disorders

One type of disorder that makes the recovery process hard is substance use disorder. This disorder is related to substance abuse or substance dependence. This includes substances that you consume to ensure relief for the short term. These substances make you disconnected from your surroundings. Being in this state for long periods makes it harder for the child/adult to recover and focus on the activities that will improve the condition.

Furthermore, substance use promotes reckless and risky behavior. In the long run, substance use and abuse will make problems even worse.

Post-traumatic stress disorder

Another disorder that makes recovery complicated is PTSD. These two disorders go hand in hand because children with BPD have experienced an extremely stressful event in the past. The same events that cause BPD are also most likely to cause PTSD. The exact reason PTSD makes it harder to recover from BPD is unknown, but there are some explanations. Having both disorders is a sign that you have survived a particularly traumatic experience.

This may cause the PTSD to refresh the BPD whenever you have flashbacks of the event; that's why the recovery process is more challenging because you have to start all over again.

Another reason is that BPD and PTSD have the same set of problems, and having double doses of the same thing can make it a lot harder to deal with. Both disorders compound the issues making it very challenging to progress toward recovery.

For instance, emotional dysregulation is a central part of BPD; it is also present in PTSD. If you have both disorders, expect a double dose of negative emotions. People with PTSD tend to avoid remembering the events that trigger it; people with BPD also avoid getting into problems that bring negative emotions. Double dose of avoidance make it even harder to recover from BPD.

Mood and Anxiety Disorders

The presence of other disorders such as depression and panic disorder also interferes with the recovery of BPD. Suppose you have either one of these disorders along with BPD. In that case, it could mean that you are highly emotional, very vulnerable, and sensitive, and you have difficulty managing your emotions.

Although we all try to avoid getting anxious by preventing the problems straight away, avoiding or not letting ourselves feel these emotions can actually make things worse. If your try to be ignorant and prevent the problems, your life becomes scary as you are not bold enough to take on the issues.

Children with depression tend to withdraw from daily activities and isolate themselves to avoid having contact with other people. However, to battle depression, you need to do the exact opposite. You need to become livelier and get yourself involved in more activities.

Depression and anxiety disorders make it harder to recover from BPD because the avoidance that goes with these disorders prevents you from doing the things that will help you recover from BPD.

Other Personality Disorders

Finally, due to other personality disorders along with BPD, it seems to interfere with the remission process from BPD. Children diagnosed with BPD along with other personality disorders are more than likely to meet BPD criteria after six years. Three anxious-fearful personality disorders that hinder the recovery of BPD are listed below:

- An avoidant personality disorder is characterized by having extreme shyness in a social environment. A child feels inadequate, fears rejection and disapproval from others, and is very sensitive to negative evaluation from others.
- A dependent personality disorder is characterized by a strong need for support or care from others. Children fear abandonment or separation from others which leads them to exhibit clinging behavior towards other people.
- An obsessive-compulsive personality disorder is characterized by being preoccupied with orderliness and control that is so extreme and pervasive that it interferes with getting things done efficiently.

Some researchers have suggested that these personality disorders are underlaid with an inhibited temperament. Children and adults with inhibited temperament tend to be anxious and cautious in a new environment, are often shy, and struggle to open up. The recovery process from BPD is challenging and requires lots of energy and personal risk. For children who are born shy and reserved, the recovery process is slower. People who are born a bit more active have a leg up in the recovery process of BPD.

If your child is shy or more reserved, it doesn't mean that he/she won't recover from BPD. What it means is that your child's recovery may be difficult, and you may have to push yourself to help your child recover.

CHAPTER 6: PROBLEMS THAT OFTEN GO ALONG WITH BORDERLINE PERSONALITY DISORDER

As discussed earlier, symptoms of BPD are very distressing. Children diagnosed with BPD often feel like there life is out of control. Having overwhelming emotions makes their life miserable, and going through it every day becomes a struggle. Unfortunately, many children with BPD have to live with this disorder and other psychiatric disorders that tend to go along with BPD. I will discuss these issues below:

Psychiatric Disorders That Often Co-Occur with BPD

BPD comes with a lot of baggage. Most children diagnosed with BPD have at least one psychiatric disorder; some have even more disorders. If your child has BPD, you may have noticed that your child also struggles with anxiety and depression. As discussed earlier, coping with multiple symptoms of different psychiatric disorders is challenging and makes recovery harder. Therefore, it is essential to know about the disorders that often go along with BPD.

Substance Use

Substance use or dependency is widespread in patients with BPD. They depend on pills and medicine to make them calm. They greatly rely on their medication, and they cannot go through the day without them. As these medicines make them numb, it gets challenging to stay on the recovery path.

Escaping and Avoiding Emotional Pain

Using substances provide an escape from emotional pain. As discussed, wanting to escape and avoid emotional pain is natural and perfectly normal. One way to get away from these feelings is simply getting away from the things causing the distress. We tend to take some time off, call a friend, or engage in an activity that will ease our minds and thoughts.

Whenever we are angry, we do the same thing, leave the place and the situation that is making us angry, and engage in something that will divert all the feelings. When we are distressed and uncomfortable, we want to get far away from these emotions and feelings.

Problems with Avoiding and Escaping Emotional Pain

Even though it is a normal desire to leave a distressing situation, you may face some negative consequences in your emotions and feelings.

The problem with preventing emotions will stop you or your child from facing the issues and solving them. The problem will stick around and will make you or your child more upset whenever it comes back. Ultimately, the patient will get caught in a cycle of avoiding the problem, and the issues will eventually pile up.

Another problem is that children with BPD are more emotional and sensitive when compared with other kids. Although there is nothing wrong with being emotional, the coping strategies that others use for these emotions do not work with your child. This is because something powerful is needed to cope with the intense emotions. As a result, not finding something that will smoothen the situation will only make things worse.

Problems with Using medication and substances for long periods

Another problem is using substances and medication to make your child calm. This will provide the solution for the short term, but in the long run, your child will be dependent on the medication to make themselves feel better. This will make them feel worse in the long term when tapering off the medications.

Another problem is that the children will likely build up a tolerance and will need to administer even more medication to help them feel better. This will increase the craving for the substance or medicine, and if the drug is suddenly stopped, they will have to face withdrawal symptoms that are likely to worsen the situation. Your child will have to go through physical pain.

Eating Disorders

Eating disorders are also prevalent in children with BPD. research shows that around 50 percent of the children with BPD also suffer from eating disorders. An eating disorder can take two forms: the food intake is restricted so much that a child/adult is underweight or bingeing and purging so much food that food is eliminated through vomiting.

Escaping and Avoiding Emotional Pain

Bingeing and purging can be used to cope with emotional distress and to relieve negative emotions. Eating is one of the common ways to soothe oneself. Even those who don't have eating disorders turn to food in times of distress or stress. Research shows that the tendency of people to lean towards eating food in times of stress explains the high rate of obesity in the United States.

Just like medication, using foods can also provide relief. Specific types of food such as candy, cakes, bread, and cookies improve mood and give temporary relaxation. Eating sugary and fatty foods activates the pleasure center of the brain and relieves stress.

Although binge eating provides temporary relief, it can become an addiction over time. Eating more and more for comfort will make the situation out of control. And if you have bulimia, eating more will make you purge more. Purging is harmful and has serious health problems.

Body Dissatisfaction

Another reason for disordered eating is body dissatisfaction.

Children with BPD often experience negative remarks about themselves, and many of the comments can be on their looks and appearance. Going through emotional abuse, they are susceptible to how they look and carry themselves. This makes the child grow up hating their body, and in their mind, thinness is the ideal body type to achieve.

The behavior that they engage in can abnormally increase or restrict their food intake. These children believe that by doing so, they will not gain weight. Purging and restricting food intake are so harmful that they can put one in life-threatening situations.

That's why body dissatisfaction is one of the reasons that eating disorders are common among children with BPD.

Sense of Control

One of the things that can be very distressing is the lack of control. If your children have BPD, they are often overwhelmed by their emotions, feelings, and behavior that is out of their control. This makes your child desperate to find solutions for this situation. An eating disorder is one way to feel that they have control over something.

Although this sense of control is actually an illusion since an eating disorder is usually out of their control. Still, purposeful purging and restricting intake to be thin gives them some sense of control.

The problem here is that this control is not accurate, and food restriction can soon spiral out of control. However, the desire to have control over oneself is a basic human need and is entirely understandable.

Depression

Many children with BPD also experience depression. It is more than just sadness. It refers to the symptoms which together can cause tremendous damage, including the following:

- Intense sadness and hopelessness.
- Loss of pleasure in formerly enjoyable activities.
- Suicidal thoughts.
- Low self-esteem.
- Appetite and sleep changes (too much or too little).
- Concentration difficulties.
- Low motivation and energy.

Depression is most likely the common disorder among children with BPD. In fact, studies have shown that 41 to 87 percent of children with BPD suffer from depression. To understand the relationship between BPD and depression, you will have to take a close look at the symptoms of BPD.

Children with BPD have difficulty having relationships with others. They experience negative emotions and have to bear negative remarks coupled with rejection and humiliation from their surroundings. They also have an intense fear of being abandoned. At last, the treatment recommended for BDP is also a demanding and challenging process.

When you look at the symptoms, you can see the reason why people with BPD feel depressed. The problems that go along with BPD are precisely the same that can lead to depression.

Bipolar Disorder

Approximately 10 percent of people with BPD are also diagnosed with bipolar disorder. Bipolar disorder is a category of disorders that share standard features. People with bipolar disorders tend to have extreme fluctuations in their moods. If your child is diagnosed with bipolar, they would feel depressed for several weeks, and suddenly their mood will light up.

They would feel on top of the world and ready to take on anything.

There are several types of bipolar disorders, but all of them involve extreme mood swings. As emotional dysfunction is widespread in children and adults with BPD, having bipolar tagging along with it is not surprising.

The Problem of Misdiagnosis

The problem with the similarities between BPD and bipolar disorder is that they both can often be confused. I have seen many people coming for their bipolar disorder, but they actually have BPD. One of the main reasons for misdiagnosis is that mood swings are both disorders' primary and common features. The fact that bipolar has further different types makes it more confusing.

Despite the confusion, there is a distinct difference between the mood swings of both disorders. The mood swings in bipolar don't occur as quickly as they appear in BPD. In bipolar disorder, a child will feel depressed for a couple of days and then experience a swift change towards an elated mood. But a child with BPD will have their mood swings in a matter of minutes or hours.

However, clinicians who are not familiar with BPD often misjudge its symptoms with bipolar disorder and misdiagnose the condition.

Another reason that children with BPD are misdiagnosed is the stigma in society. Some clinicians would instead diagnose someone with bipolar disorder in the hope that this disorder carries less stigma. I appreciate it as they don't want to stigmatize other people, but no one wants to live with the wrong diagnosis. It is my firm belief that everyone should be provided with an accurate diagnosis.

Social Anxiety Disorder

Let's take a look at social anxiety disorder. It involves intense fear of being negatively evaluated by other people in a social environment. Children with this disorder may not talk or open up easily because of the fear of being judged or humiliated by someone. These children are also hesitant to eat in front of someone or go to parties.

A symptom of social anxiety disorder that goes along with BPD is the relationship problems children with BPD face. A result of abusive, humiliating, and challenging relationships makes them anxious around new people.

If your child has had an invalidating experience in the past, they might be afraid of expressing themselves freely around other people. Your child may become less trusting of others and develop a constant fear of being in social gatherings, especially in an environment where other people may scrutinize your child.

Panic Disorder

Let's have a look at another disorder; panic disorder. In this situation, children experience recurring and unexpected panic attacks. They may experience sudden intense anxiety accompanied by specific kinds of fear, such as fear of dying or losing control of themselves.

Human bodies are hardwired in a way that responds quickly to stressful situations. It's called a 'fight-or-flight response. When faced with a threat, the human body prepares to fight or flee the situation. However, sometimes this response can misfire. When a human body is stressed out and proper care has not been taken, the body's fight-or-flight system may fire without any threat.

As there is no threat present, it is then called a panic attack. A panic attack occurs without any warning, and these attacks are out of the blue and unpredictable.

Panic attacks relate to BPD due to the nature of BPD's symptoms. Children with BPD experience heightened levels of stress. If your child has BPD, he might be more stressed than other children. An increase in stress levels over everyday things and difficulty managing the pressure can cause the body's fight-or-flight system to misfire and generate a random panic attack. In fact, researchers believe that stress, along with difficulty in managing these difficulties, increases the likelihood of panic attacks. Unfortunately, if a panic attack occurs, it will likely lead to worries and fears about panic attacks happening in the future.

Post-traumatic stress disorder

PTSD is also common among children diagnosed with BPD. It is so common in children with BPD that clinicians often suggested BPD be the form of chronic or lasting PTSD in the past. However, that narrative is no more valid as both are different disorders. Because it has long been suggested to be closely intertwined, these disorders often go hand in hand.

As discussed, PTSD and BPD can both be caused by the same set of traumatic events. For instance, childhood abuse is one of the reasons that causes BPD. Childhood abuse is also one of the traumatic events that can cause PTSD.

Therefore, children who grew up with abuse are likely to be diagnosed with both BPD and PTSD.

CHAPTER 7: HOW DO I FIND HELP FOR MY CHILD WITH BORDERLINE PERSONALITY DISORDER?

Diego wondered if he had BPD. He had always struggled with his emotions and found himself drawn towards stormy and intense relationships. He often asked himself what was wrong with him, but he never knew what it was and how to find the issue. Recently he read something on the Internet about BPD and thought that he might be suffering from this disorder. He wasn't sure what to do and how to get help as he didn't have any guidance.

If your child thinks they have BPD, it can bring a stew of emotions, fear, and confusion. Although there is help everywhere regarding BPD, finding this help is in itself a very daunting experience. In this chapter, I have described ways to find help, what kind of help is available, and what things you should focus on as you determine what is best for you or your child.

Treading Safely Through the Minefield: Internet Resources for BPD

The Internet is definitely a mixed bag when it comes to information about BPD. Although some websites provide authentic and detailed information, some websites are full of unverified sources and promote activities solely based on myths and bad advice. Choosing between these options can be a very daunting experience. It is tough to know which one to trust on the Internet. I have added some websites below that can help you on your journey with BPD.

Treatment and Research Advancements National Association for Personality Disorder (TARA NAPD) (www.tara4bpd.org)

This organization is dedicated to helping children diagnosed with BPD. It enables the family members of the diagnosee to find help and accurate information about BPD. It also gives options about the available treatment plans. It is one of the esteemed and dedicated organizations that are bent on improving awareness and understanding of BPD. The primary and essential goals of this organization are:

- Making the public more aware of the facts of the disorder.

- Encouraging institutions that fund research to provide more money for the studies and surveys on BPD.
- TARA NAPD is also dedicated to making effective treatments readily available across the United States.

This website is full of helpful information for the users and family members of the BPD patient. One of the valuable services on the website is the referral program for the treatment programs and clinicians offering treatment, which are known to be promising and scientifically correct. You can be confident about the treatment plan that this website refers to.

National Education Alliance for BPD(NEA-BPD) (www.borderlinepersonalitydisorder.com)

Just like TARA NAPD, the NEA-BPD is also dedicated to raising awareness about BPD. This website provides education on BPD and promotes research on the cause and treatment of the disorder. This website has a twelve-week class that includes information on BPD and teaches skills and advice to the family member of the diagnosee so they can have improved interactions with their BPD children.

This website also provides access to other people who are also dealing with similar problems. These classes here are available in the United States and across Canada.

NEA-BPD provides the latest research on BPD. This website also boasts reputable information on BPD.

The Borderline Sanctuary (www.mhsanctuary.com/borderline)

This website is an excellent resource for information and education about BPD. It also includes links to clinicians and researchers who have dedicated their work towards BPD. It also has chat rooms and a communal program so that people with similar problems can get in touch or have treatment referrals.

BPD Central (www.bpdcentral.com)

This website is primarily geared towards the family members of the person who is diagnosed with BPD. It gives information and educational material on BPD and has various online support groups for families of adults or children diagnosed with BPD.

Behavioral Tech LLC (www.behavioraltech.org)

This website provides services that give referrals to treatment providers throughout the world. There is also video and other material about BPD on this website that can be helpful for parents whose children have BPD.

Other Ways to Find Information on BPD

Nowadays, the Internet is one of the best sources to find BPD information about reputable and trustworthy websites. However, there are still some ways where you can find more information on BPD. For instance, many books give detailed explanations and information on BPD. These books include autobiography, research, and thesis, self-hep books. It depends on the kind of information you need, and any of these books can help you find that information.

Another great way to obtain information is to talk to a local psychological professor. It's better if someone close to you is studying in a related psychological program, they can get in touch with the professors there and get you a better insight. The obvious way to get accurate and denounce information is to get in touch with a BPD expert. They have enough resources and expertise to help you out with any information or problem.

CHAPTER 8: WHAT KINDS OF TREATMENT ARE AVAILABLE FOR CHILDREN WITH BPD?

Two primary treatments are available for BPD patients:
- Psychological treatments.
- Medications.

Psychological treatments involve meeting a mental health professional regularly and explaining the struggles your child has to go through daily. These professionals will help identify the root of problems and give advice on how to address the issues.

Medication treatment involves meeting a psychiatrist, getting an evaluation on the medication that may work in your child's case, and receiving a prescription. The meeting with psychiatrists has to be held regularly to evaluate the progress and look out for any side effects of the medicine your child is consuming.

I have added a detailed discussion below about the treatments you may need when finding help for you or your child.

Psychological Treatments

There may be various treatment options available for BPD, depending on where you live. These treatments differ in intensity, how many (hours per week), and how long they last. Generally, intense treatments last for shorter periods when compared with less intensive therapies. The most intensive treatment typically has round the clock monitoring system. Intensive treatments are used when there is a risk that patients are in a state of crisis and risk of serious self-harm. Most often, the goal is to help the patient get through an immediate problem.

The downside of intensive treatment is that it takes people out of their regular routine. Although it sounds good to get away from the work routine, it can be a problem as it prevents children with BPD from dealing with issues themselves. As this treatment is very intensive and challenging, it is recommended that they should last for short periods.

The less intensive treatment involves going to the hospital for several hours per day, for several days per week. This enables the patient to go home at night and take part in some of the routine activities. These treatments often help children make the transition from the inpatient unit to the outpatient unit.

These programs are more popular and are more readily available.

The least intensive treatment and the best-known treatment is outpatient care. For most children and adults with BPD, outpatient treatment involves between one to five hours of therapy in a week. This treatment includes one or two therapy sessions in a week. These therapy sessions can be in the form of a group. Some common types of therapy include:

- Cognitive-behavioral therapy (CBT) is a treatment that helps children with BPD learn new skills and helps them manage their emotions. CBT is a structured form of therapy with a primary focus on figuring out the patterns that aren't working well. CBT often includes home-based assignments through which children learn new skills.
- Dialectical behavior therapy (DBT) is a specific form of CBT that combines with the elements of CBT discussed above with strategies that help children with BPD accept themselves, their lives, and the people around them.
- Psychological therapy helps children with BPD figure out what they do and where these patterns are coming

from. Psychodynamic therapies focus on the patient's growing experience.

Although all therapies and treatment plans are helpful, experts suggest that the most effective treatment is the least intensive treatment. This basically means that the treatment that is embedded with daily life proves to be more efficient.

Medications

In addition to the psychological treatments, certain medications may help with the symptoms of BPD. Experts suggest that medication should be used along with psychological treatments as medicine alone cannot do the trick.

What to Expect When You Meet with a Mental Health Professional

Many mental health professionals provide psychological assessments and treatment plans for BPD. All mental health professionals such as clinical psychologists and psychiatrists are trained to provide assessment and treatment plans. However, only psychiatrists can give the medication for the symptoms of BPD.

Psychological Assessments

When getting a thorough and detailed psychological assessment, you can expect to be asked many questions. Questions can be about your child's mood, thoughts, emotions, problematic behaviors, and personal likes and dislikes. Many of the questions revolve around the symptoms your child has had to deal with. Typical questions that are asked are:

- Are your child's relationships stormy or chaotic?
- Do your child's emotions or moods change a lot?
- Has your child ever deliberately hurt himself without meaning to kill himself?
- Is your child unsure of who they are or what they are really like?

Assessment can also include filling out forms and questionnaires about the symptoms, mood, or anything personal.

Individual Therapy

In individual therapy, the first few sessions involve the get-to-know phase.

The therapist will ask many questions about the reason for getting treatment, current issues, and how long you have been dealing with these issues. Many therapists will also be interested to know about your child's past and struggles.

Once the therapists get to know you well, they will probably develop a treatment plan and discuss the treatment goals and the primary focus of the sessions. There will be some discussion before the treatment plan, so both the parties agree on the treatment plan, and there are no reservations.

Group Therapy

Group therapies are diverse and have different goals and purposes. Your child's role in the group will vary according to the task they are given. Depending on the type of group your child is entering, the way your child is introduced to the group may differ. If your child is joining an enhancing skill group, they might be asked to introduce themselves briefly. If your child is entering a psychodynamic group, the introductions may be formal, and your child may be asked to provide more information.

Medication Treatment

Suppose your child sees a doctor or therapist that monitors their medication and regularly checks them up for any side effects.

In that case, your child can probably expect some talking in the session, although the session will be fewer and shorter. Initial sessions with the therapist are generally longer as they learn about your child and their symptoms; afterward, the session typically lasts from fifteen to thirty minutes. The focus of these meetings is the symptoms that are being dealt with. That being said, therapists who give a prescription of medicine can also provide psychological treatment. If your child has any problem or issue that they feel can be discussed with the therapist, your child should ask without any hesitation.

Specific Steps for Getting Help

I have added some specific steps that you can use for getting help for your child with BPD.

1) *Find a Mental Health Professional with Training and Experience in Treating BPD*

The websites I have mentioned are excellent places to start looking, as you can get many referrals. Other options also include calling a local hospital for a mental health professional. Always check out the professional's credibility and, if possible, get in touch with their previous patients to get feedback.

2) *Get a Thorough Psychological Assessment and Diagnosis*

It is essential to get a proper diagnosis from a trained professional. When people start to read about the symptoms, they feel that they are suffering from these symptoms. There is also a term used for this phenomenon, 'medical student syndrome.' It is never a good idea to self-diagnose and always seek the guidance of a professional.

3) *Ask Questions and Discuss These Recommendations with the Right Person*

The best way to ensure that your child is getting the proper treatment is to ensure that both the parties involved are the right fit for each other. So, ask essential questions regarding information, problems, queries. Important questions that you should ask are:

- What are your credentials, your background education, and your expertise?
- How long have you been treating children diagnosed with BPD?
- Do you have specialized treatment or training for children with BPD?
- What kind of treatment is provided (such as cognitive-behavioral, DBT, or psychodynamic)?
- What types of treatment are available (individual therapy, group therapy, family therapy, or medications)? Will I have access to more than one type?
- How long does treatment usually last?
- How many hours per week does this treatment involve?
- What will my child be expected to do in this treatment?
- What is the cost of the treatment? Do you accept private insurance, Medicare, or Medicaid?

CHAPTER 9: DEALING WITH SUICIDAL THOUGHTS

If you have come this far in the book, you probably will ask what you can do to manage your issues. We have talked about everything in detail regarding BPD, the problems, the treatments, etc. Even if your child is getting the treatment, it is essential to know something to help your child manage their emotions.

After careful consideration, I have included this chapter because if your child harms themselves and takes their life, there is no point in learning new skills. Just know that if your child has suicidal thoughts, they are currently in a lot of pain. All they need at this moment is the support, love, and care of the parents. The goals and aims of this chapter are to help your child learn how to cope with suicidal thoughts.

Steps to Take If You Are Feeling Suicidal

If your child is thinking about self-harm and suicide regularly, it may be very tough to break this habit. This is because your child is actually feeling soothed. In their mind, they will escape all of the problems through suicide.

This thought has become a reflex because your child's mind immediately thinks about suicide if anything wrong happens. It is challenging to change a reflex-like that.

I have added steps below that the patient can take if his/her mind is plagued with suicidal thoughts.

Get Away from "Lethal Means"

When you feel that your child is thinking of harming themselves, it is best to remove any objects used for this purpose. Make sure that all the lethal means are removed and put away safely. The idea here is your child is far less likely to harm themselves if there are no lethal objects nearby. Some of the things to be put out safely are:

- Medicines should be put under lock as your child can overdose on them.
- Put the knives and forks in a secret or hidden place.
- Don't let your child buy things unsupervised.
- Keep a sharp eye on the objects your child is using and check out their room from time to time to see for any lethal objects.

Think About What You Really Want

If your children have suicidal thoughts, it is suggested that they divert their minds towards the things they really want. Things that will make them feel better about themselves. Most people who attempt suicide say that they do this to escape their emotions.

Make your child believe that these problems can be solved without sustaining any harm. Start by taking the following steps:

1) Tell your child to figure out the problem whenever they have suicidal thoughts; you will get thoughts about suicide when dealing with the situation.

2) Help your child figure out what they want. Find a way to make your child feel better for the time being.

3) The next step is to help your child figure out what can be done instead of sustaining harm. Look around for coping mechanisms that can be used.

4) Make your child understand that suicide is not an easy way out and it is only a temporary solution. Life is full of surprises, and you may not know if the surprise is just around the corner.

There are also many other ways and solutions to get out of pain; you just have to help your child find it. Consult a therapist for any help and advice, call a friend or family member if you need emotional support.

Change the Situation

You would be amazed by how your child's mood will change once the environment around them changes. Just don't only plan on going out somewhere; just do it. When in different places, your child will admire the new sights, smells, and tastes around. This will allow your child to have a different perspective to view the world.

Below are some places that you should consider going to with your child:

- Mall.
- Coffee shop.
- Busy Park.
- Beach.
- Mountains
- Fitness center.
- Library.

- Zoo.
- Relative's home.
- Friend's home.

Think About Reasons to Stay Alive

Another skill that can come in handy is to make your child feel about the reasons they have to live for. I have added some of the reasons that your child should live for:

- Beliefs that you will ultimately be able to make your life better and solve your problems in other ways.
- Concerns that you could hurt your family by killing yourself.
- Concerns that you would hurt your children, partner, friends, pets, or others whom you care about if you killed yourself.
- Fears of dying.
- Fears of failing in your suicide attempt and being worse off as a result (being paralyzed, damaging your body, and having medical problems like chronic pain, for example).
- Fears of pain.
- Moral or religious objections to suicide.
- Fears of disapproval from other people.

- Fears of something terrible happening to you (like going to hell) if you were to kill yourself.

It can be beneficial for your child to have reasons not to think of harming themselves. Take a look through the list and see if any of the reasons are essential to your child. Afterward, try to come up with more reasons that you think can help your child.

Take Action and Challenge Hopeless Thinking

Researchers have given their opinion that hopeless thoughts about the future lead to suicidal thinking and behavior. Children with these thoughts think of themselves as a hopeless cause. They firmly believe that adverse events will happen, and there is very little chance of any good happening. The best way to deal with this is to make your child take action now and push them to avoid acting hopeless.

One skill that your child can use is to start acting opposite of what they are thinking. For instance, if you feel frustrated and angry and want to yell at someone, the opposite is to be kind to that person. This strategy cannot be used in all scenarios. For example, if you feel better and calm, you don't have to use this strategy. Using this strategy is recommended when your mind is clouded with hopeless thoughts.

Whenever your child has hopeless thoughts, you should make your child busy by having them call their friend or relative.

Taking even small steps can improve the mood and give hope to do things for a change. Make your child have an open perspective on what is happening around them, and make sure that they are paying attention to the small steps that are important and making a difference.

Let the Thoughts Come and Go

Another valuable skill to tackle these thoughts is to simply help your child with having suicidal thoughts and let them go. This concept is based on the idiom 'go in one ear and out the other.' The idea is to have these thoughts but not act on them. We all have various thoughts on which we don't act. Thoughts are just thoughts, and they can be compelling. But you have complete freedom to have thoughts and simply let them through.

Imagine that you are lying in a large green field and looking up at the sky. It's a peaceful day, warm and sunny, with a slight breeze. In the sky, you see some large, billowing white clouds floating by. Imagine that your thoughts are written on each cloud, watch the clouds as they float by. Imagine your thoughts as a cloud. Don't follow any one of the clouds; just see them pass through.

Use Any of the Emotional Coping Skills Provided in the Next Chapter

As discussed, children with BPD have suicidal thoughts because they believe it is an exit from their life's emotional pain and misery. For all we know, those who commit suicide have to feel the same thing till eternity. To live the life you want, you have to stay alive and fight for it. If you want your child to feel better, I recommend trying all skills and sticking with those which work. We will have a look at skills in the next section.

CHAPTER 10: COPING WITH YOUR EMOTIONS

This section is all about the useful skills that your children can use to manage their intense emotions and help themselves get through difficult times. Although your children can help themselves with these skills, there is no evidence that self-help is enough; they probably need your help.

Skills You Can Use to Cope with Emotions

Children with BPD frequently struggle with emotions. Being too emotional is not the problem, but coping with the emotions is. With the help of this guide, your child can learn ways to manage their emotions effectively.

Practice Accepting Your Emotions and Your Situation Right Now

One of the simplest yet hardest ways for your child to deal with the emotions is to accept the feelings that they are experiencing. I insist that accepting emotions requires hard work, and it is something more important than achieving it. For instance, it is not like passing an exam and being done with a course; instead, it is like cleaning your home, and still, you have to do it again.

Accepting is the process of stopping the struggle, suppressing, avoiding, escaping, or getting rid of the emotions. Instead, your child simply has to leave the emotion there. If something bad happens and you feel bad, you have to feel bad as it happened, just like if you felt happy after something pleasant happened. Accepting is like being in a tug of war with the monster. You just have to drop the rope and allow the monster to be.

Distraction

Sometimes patients with BPD should focus their attention on something else if they feel down due to intense negative emotions. This will help them as they will get their mind off whatever is troubling them at that moment. Your BPD child can distract himself in many ways:

- Tell your child to count backward from 100, or start from 115 and keep on subtracting 7 until they reach 3.
- Do something that will keep their minds busy such as puzzles, word games, video games, or Sudoku.
- Tell your child to do something that will need their complete attention and focus. Tell them to pay attention to that work.

- Tell your child to do something that they enjoy and feel happy doing.
- Tell your child to imagine themselves in nice and comfy places such as vacation spots, or tell them to imagine themselves in a fantasy.
- Listening to loud and energetic music can also lift up the mood.

Just make sure that the distraction your child is using is not harmful or hurtful. Ensure that the activities they are engaging in are healthy and not adverse in the long run.

Relaxation Strategies

Most treatments for anxiety disorders involve skills that help people to relax, and for many people, this technique is quite helpful. This skill does not only help to manage anxiety but also helps manage other emotions, such as anger. Two of the most common relaxation techniques are muscle relaxation and diaphragmatic breathing. Simply slowing your breathing down is also very helpful in these situations.

Make sure that while practicing this skill, your child is not stressed or anxious.

Progressive Muscle Relaxation

Progressive muscle relaxation, or PMR for short, is a technique your child can use to reduce tension and anxiety.

Your child can do this sitting up, laying down, or standing up, but it is suggested that your child should be lying down.

PMR basically is the tensing and relaxing of body muscles. The idea is to purposefully tense body muscles and relax them after a very short period. Muscles need to be tightened a lot during this activity. Important things for the activity are mentioned below:

1. The first thing is to find a place to do this activity. Then decide whether to start from head or toes and work your way accordingly up or down.
2. Let's say you are starting from your toes. Bring your complete attention towards your toes. Curl the toes towards the inside until you feel the tension in the toes. Hold them in this position for 5 to 10 seconds.
3. Relax your toes after five to ten seconds. Notice the relaxation, warmth, or any other feelings in the toes.

4. Then move up to the ankles and do the same technique. Create tension in the ankles for five to ten seconds and then relax them.
5. Keep doing this and work your way up to the head.

There are two main goals for this activity:

1. To help you notice the difference between the feeling of having tense muscles and having relaxed muscles.
2. To help you feel more relaxed. People often say that they feel at least 50 percent more relaxed after they do this exercise.

Diaphragmatic Breathing

This activity is also helpful for your child to deal with emotions such as anxiety, anger, or frustration. It involves breathing slowly and deliberately through your diaphragm. Try to take full and deep breaths.

Your child needs to practice this skill in a quiet place where other people won't interrupt them. Tell your child to sit in an upright position and put one hand on the chest and the other on the abdomen. After this, ask them to breathe normally and notice which hand is moving more. If the hand on the chest is moving more, then your child is not breathing through the diaphragm.

Tell your child to continue breathing and draw air into their lungs through the abdomen. Make them look at this until their lower hand is moving more than the upper hand. Tell them to deepen their breathing slowly.

This activity is helpful as breathing through the abdomen gives a better exchange of oxygen and carbon dioxide. It also slows you down and gives you something to focus on.

Slowing Down Your Breathing

The final activity related to relaxation is just to slow down your breathing. Tell your child to take shallow, quick breaths when they are upset or anxious. Tell them to focus on slowing down their breathing as this will also give them something to divert their mind towards. Tell your child to take a deep breath and count to six, then exhale out. They can also slowly increase the number of seconds they hold their breath.

Mindful Walking Meditation

Mindful walking meditation is a discipline. It's a lifestyle that requires devotion, focus, consistency, courage, awareness, and self-confidence. It is a combination of two words, i.e., mindful walking and walking meditation. Mindful walking means using walking as a source to reach your set goals.

That means you have to assign yourself a goal, and by setting short milestones, you have to reach your ultimate destiny through walking. Walking meditation, on the other hand, is different to mindful walking.

In the latter case, you don't need a set goal or target, but you will be self-aware about your walking pattern, each and every step you take, and your breathing pattern. It allows you to focus on your inner self. That is why it's called 'meditation'.

Mindful walking meditation combines the benefits of mindful walking and walking meditation. In this process, you set a specific goal and divide it into short milestones. You also focus on your walking and breathing pattern to coordinate your mindful walking meditation, body, and spirit. This process helps you walk through your pain barrier, and you push your limits a little further daily. Mindful walking meditation is a great way to start a change process in your life, and it makes you more self-aware. So, you will have all the benefits of mindfulness and meditation.

Mindfulness has proven benefits against the most prevalent symptoms of BPD.

Better endurance:
Endurance is a muscle's capacity to work for a prolonged period of time. In psychology, endurance is the mind's ability to cope with stress for a longer duration. Mindful walking meditation helps in increasing mental and physical endurance.

 Physical endurance is increased by repetitive and sustained loading on muscles involved in walking and balancing.

Mindful walking meditation increases the blood supply in working muscles, and eventually, the muscles are adapted to the imposed stress. As you push your limits, the capacities of muscles are also increased.

Mental endurance is increased by enhancing the brain's capacity to overcome your fears. The desensitization process of mindful walking meditation allows us to become less receptive to pain and negativity. So, mindful walking meditation is very helpful to give you more endurance and make you more agile.

Balance and coordination:

The meditational benefits of this process allow you to find the balance between mindful walking meditation, body, and spirit. It is the basis of holistic medicine. This balance is crucial because it allows you to bring a permanent change in your life by increasing the body's adaptive responses towards imposed stress. In mindful walking meditation, you try to be aware of your breathing and walking pattern, which allows you to coordinate your movements.

People who suffer from coordination issues (old age population) can find mindful walking meditation really helpful in treating these issues.

Increased strength:

When you spend hours on your couch, eat junk food, and remain inactive throughout your day, your muscles become weak, and your bones become fragile. You lose your strength, and even the activities of daily living can be very damaging for you. So, in that case, you will need mindful walking meditation to boost the strength in your body. Mindful walking meditation allows you to come out of your lazy zone, and daily physical activity allows you to regain your lost strength.

 All that debate was about physical strength, but you also need mental strength to overcome your fears and bring a permanent change in your life. Mindful walking meditation allows you to bring a slow and steady change in your life, which is easier to maintain than an abrupt and short-lived change in your lifestyle. Increased mental and physical strength can help BPD patients to cope with negativity and impulsiveness.

Better control of your thoughts:

It is well-established that depression and anxieties are thought processes that can be altered.

Actually, the biggest source of depression and anxieties are negative thoughts imposed by personal and environmental triggers.

These disorders are not developed in a single day, and it is an ongoing process, so mindful walking meditation helps you control your thought processes through its meditational benefits. When you are aware of your walking and breathing patterns, your mindful walking meditation works in a more coordinated pattern, so the distorted thoughts in your brain become more organized with time, which is essential to bring a permanent change in your life.

Pleasant mood:

Nature and walking, when combined, influence your mood in a very strong way because of the benefits associated with both of them. The natural environment brings peace and harmony to your life. In this machinic world, we are very far from reality, and our bodies crave to become closer to nature. Walk, on the other hand, helps you to synchronize the natural movements in your body. Mindful walking meditation specifically involves the combined benefits of mindfulness and meditation.

It helps in organizing your thought and making you more receptive to nature's call. You become desensitized towards negative thoughts and negative people, which eventually boosts your mood.

It is essential to prevent or treat depression and anxiety. I found mindful walking meditation very useful to manage my stress responses.

Self-confidence:

Mindful walking meditation involves a consistent change in your life habits. You set a goal and divide it into short milestones.

This process is unique when it comes to mindful walking meditation because it combines with better self-awareness. They say that a person who knows his own worth can prove his worth to others. So, by completing your daily targets and tracking them properly, you actually boost confidence in your own self. You know that you are getting stronger day by day, and you realize that you have lost much because of your self-centered fears and anxieties. It brings drastic changes in your personal and social lives, and you become more confident in your social network.

Physical wellness:

Wellness is an umbrella term that incorporates physical, mental, spiritual, and emotional wellness. Physical wellness is a feeling of utmost health in one's body. It is a state in which a person is free from any kind of disease. Optimal health requires physical, mental, emotional, and spiritual health.

Here lies the importance of holistic medicine, which incorporates the balance between mindful walking meditation body and spirit. Mindful walking meditation helps in achieving optimal physical health by increasing the efficiency of our muscles, cardiovascular system, nervous and digestive system, and overall performance and stamina.

Mental wellness:

Mindful walking meditation is crucial for optimal mental health because of its meditational impacts. It allows you to become aware of your mental and cognitive capacities. It allows you to cope with depression and anxieties, and other symptoms of BPD. The increased awareness of self because of mindful walking meditation is an important factor behind its popularity.

Spiritual wellness:

Regardless of religion or religious beliefs, spirituality is a process of knowing nature. It allows you to find the hidden secrets of the natural environment around you and how it coordinates with your life.

Mindful walking meditation allows you to be closer to your natural environment, which is by far the most affected entity of this digital world.

Our bodies crave nature because of our innate responses. My pro tip to you guys is to try mindful walking meditation in an open and natural environment. With time, you will be able to focus on your walking and breathing pattern, increasing your awareness of the surrounding environment.

Bird chirps blows of fresh air, and green trees will positively impact your spiritual health. All these benefits of mindful walking can reduce the prevalence of suicidal thoughts in BPD patients.

Emotional wellness:

Emotional well-being is by far the most important but most underrated benefit of mindful walking meditation. It requires a great internal and external support circle, positivity, motivation, and self-confidence to become emotionally stable. Life is really tough, and you can feel depressed or anxious in several situations.

However, you have enough coping abilities; you will come out of that state. The duration of your comeback will depend upon your emotional wellness. Mindful walking meditation helps in desensitizing your mind towards negativity and naysayers.

You become emotionally stable eventually, and your motivation becomes unshakable. This is the state of true self-awareness, and you will know your own strengths. BPD patients can control their emotions in a better way when they start mindful activities on a regular basis.

CHAPTER 11: ACTIVITIES

Activity 1: How can you predict the consequence of your actions?

BPD patients often fail to comprehend the consequences that their actions will cause. You may know that you will get in trouble if you break a specific rule. However, you are still intimidated to break the rule. If you can predict the consequences that the specific actions will cause, you can save yourself from getting into trouble. It is relatively easy to predict the consequences of your actions. However, you will have to practice the activities that I have included. Having the ability to predict other people's reactions towards your actions helps you modify and control your actions.

Cecily's teacher gave her a list of words for her to spell. It was a routine exercise that took place every Monday. The teacher would take a test every Friday to assess the progress of the class.

Cecily was given the list so she could learn to spell new words. However, she failed to learn the spelling on Monday as she was busy watching her favorite show.

The next day, she failed again to learn as she had to go to her dance class. After the dance session, she ate her dinner and did math homework before going to bed. She didn't make time to practice the spellings that her teacher gave her.

On Wednesday, Cecily only needed 15 to 30 minutes to learn the spelling. However, both her parents were very busy that day and couldn't make time to help her learn. On Thursday, she couldn't learn and practice spellings because her cousins came over, and she spent the whole day playing.

On Friday, she failed her test and got an 'F' as she scored twenty out of twenty-five spellings wrong. Her teacher asked her to get the result signed by her parents due to the poor marks achieved. When she gave the test to her mother to get it signed, her mother was shocked at her poor performance because Cecily was good at this subject. Her mother inquired Cecily about the result and asked, "what happened." To which Cecily replied, "I don't know." Her mother then said." You know very well about it, don't you?"

I want you to take some time and think if you have ever got a poor grade because you were busy and couldn't make time to prepare and learn. I want you to tell me what happened that day.

_____

_____

_____

_____

Tasks for you

Before acting, you should not rush with your decision. Instead, take a second and think about the consequences your action will have. Anticipate the reaction of grown-ups when they see your action. I have designed a simple exercise that will help you in your behavioral modification.

Write down three things that can cause your parents to hug you.

1) _____

2) _____

3) _____

Write three things that can cause punishment or can cause your parents to yell at you.

1) _____

2) _____

3) _____

Write down three things that will make your teacher give you a good grade.

1) _____

2) _____

3) _____

Write down three things that can make others say 'thank you' in response.

1)
___

2)
___

3)
___

Activity 2: Learning patience

Children diagnosed with BPD show impulsive behavior. They don't like to sit and wait. They want to get done with things immediately. They find it difficult to wait for the things they want; for example, rather than having a larger cookie later, they would prefer to have a small cookie right now. If you show patience, you can enjoy a bigger cookie. Patience is a fundamental trait to have, as it helps you become more stable and reasonable.

Rachel was feeling very hungry; she didn't want to wait for the dinner to be served. Her mother was cooking her favorite dish. She was cooking meatballs and pasta, but she was also busy with her phone. Rachel was very annoyed as she had to wait longer for the food to get ready.

"When will the food be ready," asked Rachel. She knew very well that it was not a good habit to interrupt her mom while she was with someone on the phone. "Twenty minutes, honey," her mother replied. Rachel then waited 20 minutes and was getting impatient. After 20 minutes she went to the kitchen and saw her mother still on the phone and the meal was not prepared.

Rachel then said to her mother, "I am starving. You can talk later on the phone." Rachel's mother nodded her head to remain silent. Rachel was not putting up with her mother, and she knew her mother was also getting angry at her. Rachel then shouted, "I need my dinner right now! I am starving."

Rachel's mother gave her a furious gaze. She put down her phone and said, "what is wrong with you? Can't you wait a little bit more? It's not like you will collapse immediately. If you behave like this again, you will remain hungry tonight."

Rachel went back after this outburst with her mom. She was outraged and thought her mother was the meanest mom in the world.

Have you ever faced a similar scenario? Tell us your story below.

_____
_____
_____
_____

Tasks for you

Has someone ever told you to show patience and sit down silently?

BPD patients have to listen to this phrase frequently as they are impatient. Adults diagnosed with BPD also face a similar issue. You are annoyed when you are stuck in a traffic jam, and everyone is honking and yelling at each other. Adults with BPD may also be annoyed when they see their computers slow and stuck. This means that older people with BPD also get impatient sometimes.

Many people like to get done with things and don't like to wait. I have mentioned five things below that need patience. If you know five more things that can't be done, immediately write them below.

- Getting old
- Birthday every year
- Appointment for a doctor
- Gradually learning new skills
- Waiting for plants to grow into trees

1. —
2. —
3. —
4. —
5. —

I have included an activity for you. This activity will help you to be patient.

Patience box

Take an old shoebox to make a patience box. You can decorate it if you want. Take a piece of paper and write down things which you can do while waiting. For example, you can write that you will draw flowers in a book while waiting for dinner to get ready. You can also ask your parents and siblings to make a smart list of exciting activities. Then in the future, when you are getting annoyed while waiting, you can take a relaxing breath and reach to your patience box. Take out the list and choose an activity that makes you excited. Patience is a great trait to have. I have designed an activity that will assist you in learning patience. You have to practice it a few times and try to stay calm when doing the exercise. Acquiring patience will help you overcome your hyperactive zone.

Activity 3: Know how to follow the rules

Children are expected to follow hundreds of different rules. You may know about the rules about social engaging, eating, and riding the bicycle safely. The important thing is remembering to follow the rules. You know for a fact that that you have to follow the rules everywhere. However, you may get in trouble when you don't remember to follow the rules. The trouble you get into depends on the rule you break.

Mia was always stubborn when it came to following rules. She always tried to remain awake when her mother specifically asked her to sleep. As a result of sleeping late, Mia was late for school as she was sleeping when it was time to prepare for school.

Mia had a bad habit of delaying things even at school. She never listens to her teacher and doesn't bother to follow the school rules. Mia didn't like to participate in class and always sat beside the window. Her teacher didn't like her attitude at all.

As she was constantly breaking the rules and never listened to her teacher. As a result, her recess was blocked, and she had to do her classwork in the recess period.

Mia always enjoyed the recess break and thought that her teacher was mean by blocking her free time.

Caroline didn't want to go with her teacher when she was asked for. She would rather sit beside the window, and her teacher never liked it.

When her teacher wanted to punish her by blocking her recess, she always wanted to go outside and never wanted to stay in class.

If you have been in a similar situation, write down a few words about it below.

_____
_____
_____
_____

Tasks for you

The best way to remember the rules is to talk about them frequently. In the chart that I have added below, you can find five rules.

Rule	Result of breaking the rule
It is a bad habit to take other people's things without their permission.	
Always chew your food before swallowing and keep your mouth closed.	
Always wash your hand thoroughly before eating anything.	
Always be punctual in completing the homework.	
Refrain yourself from using curse words.	

All you have to do is fill up the free space next to them about the suspected result if you feel that a particular rule is broken. What will the troubles be that you get into if you break them? Afterward, write down five rules of your own and the results you believe will happen as a result of that.

Parents and teachers may have structured different rules for you. This is beneficial for you as by following these rules, you will keep yourself away from trouble.

I have included the chart below that you can use to keep track of such rules. Take a print of the chart and fill it in accordingly. Seek guidance from parents or teachers, so you better know about the consequences of breaking those rules.

Rule	Consequence

One important thing that you always have to account for is to talk to your parents and teachers. Talk to them about the rules and ask them why it is essential for you to follow these rules. When they see you struggling and learning to change yourself, they will feel proud of you, love your efforts, and most importantly, always back you in these situations.

Activity 4: You can have a peaceful family

Every family can face problems in getting along with each other, but these issues can be solved. Regular meetings among the family members give them a chance to say what's on their minds and help to find solutions to the problems.

There was lots of yelling in Justin's home. Justin's mom would yell at him for being loud and bringing his muddy shoes into the house, and she would also scream at her children for talking back to her. Justin's parents also yelled at each other sometimes over the small things.

The issue was so provoked that his parents decided to seek services from a family counselor. The counselor told them that they needed to communicate with each other in a better way. He said that yelling was stressful for them and kept them away from being a happy family. The counselor advised them to have regular family meetings and that they should have clear rules. Some rules he suggested were:

- A parent should head the meeting. A session should never last more than 30 minutes.

- Each person has to write down something and talk about it with the family.
- Everyone will share their problems, but they will not yell, blame, or interrupt each other.
- Discussion should be ended with two possible solutions for a problem.
- They can also plan activities or spend some fun time together.
- Each family member has to say at least one appreciating thing about another member in the group.

Have your family ever had family meetings at your home? What happened in those meetings?

_____
_____
_____
_____

Tasks for you

If you are also facing distressing situations and arguments in your home, consider having family meetings. These sessions usually work best when they are conducted regularly, on a particular day in a week.

I want you to write down five problems that you want to discuss in a family meeting.

1. _____

2. _____

3. _____

4. _____

5. _____

Write down five things other than the already-mentioned problems you would want to discuss in a family meeting.

1. _____

2. _____

3.
_____

4.
_____

5.
_____

I want you to show this activity to your parents and ask them to arrange family meetings regularly. Even if there is no yelling or arguments in your home, family meetings will help family members communicate better with each other. It helps in bringing the whole family close to each other.

These meetings are a success if they are appropriately organized. You can make copies of the page I have added below. Ask your parents to fill this form in before starting the meeting.

What will be the time for the meeting?

Start: End:

Who will run the family meeting?
_____

Things we will talk about:

1. _____

2. _____

3. _____

4. _____

Activity 5: You can get help when you need it

Being a kid with BPD can be hard sometimes. You can have problems related to health, school work, friends. But no matter what you are going through, talking about the things that bother you is always a great idea. Some kids like to discuss problems with their parents, but some prefer to speak with their counselor, teacher, grandparents, or a friend.

Harry was a happy kid. He liked his home and enjoyed spending time with his friends. Harry also loved to play football. One morning, his dad said that he needed to talk to the whole family and his dad requested everyone to gather at the dining table.

"My company is laying off people, and I'm one of them. It might be a while until I find a stable job," Harry's father said.

Harry was confused and asked if they were going to be poor.

Harry's dad smiled and said they wouldn't be poor, but they would have to make some changes.

They needed to cut their expenses which meant no family trips until he could find a job. Harry's dad said that they would have to stop buying unnecessary things. He took a deep breath and said they might have to move to another city to find a job.

Harry didn't like the idea of moving and said that he loved it here with his friends and he enjoyed playing football here. Harry was not comfortable with the idea of moving into a new place.

His father told him to calm down as moving to another city was just another possibility. Harry's father wanted his family to be mentally prepared for anything.

Have you ever faced a big family problem that made you upset? Is there any person with whom you talk about the problems you face?

_____
_____
_____
_____

Tasks For You

When there is a problem that you cannot solve on your own, the best possible scenario is to talk with someone. You can ponder over the solution offered by someone and can try using it along with your own ideas.

Below are some situations that I have added for you. What advice would you give to a kid who is facing a similar scenario?

William's mom is ill and is in hospital. William is worried that his mom's situation will not improve and that she may even die. What advice do you have for William?

_____
_____
_____
_____

Vettel's bike was stolen. His dad told him to lock up his bike properly when he got home, but he forgot to lock up his bike that day. What advice would you give to Vettel?

_____

_____

_____

_____

Amanda was having a hard time seeing the whiteboard in class. She didn't like to wear eyeglasses, so she didn't tell anyone about her problem. She would squint her eyes to see the board, but it wasn't helpful and often caused headaches. What advice would you give Amanda?

_____

_____

_____

_____

I want you to write the name of four people from whom you can ask for help. Write their names below and add a reason why you are confident in seeking their help:

1) _____

2) _____

3) _____

4) _____

My final request…

Being a smaller author, reviews help me tremendously! It would mean the world to me if you could leave a review.

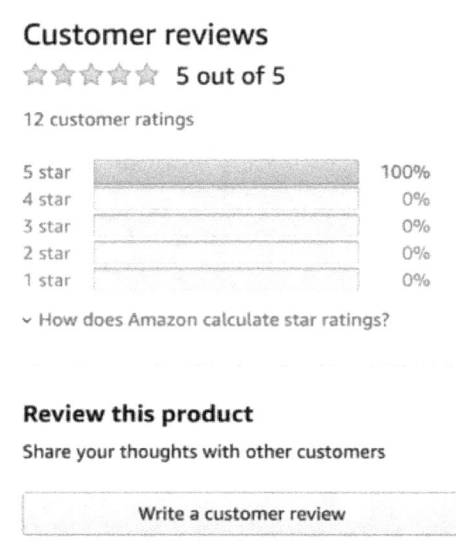

If you liked reading this book and learned a thing or two, please let me know!

It only takes 30 seconds but means so much to me!

Thank you and I can't wait to see your thoughts.

CONCLUSION

The Diagnostic and Statistical Manual of Mental Disorders is like a recipe book used by mental health professionals to list essential psychological or emotional problems. Two primary psychiatric disorders listed in this book are personality disorders and clinical disorders. According to this book, BPD is a psychiatric disorder that fits in the category of personality disorders.

It is essential to know something about the history of BPD. In the 19th century, people used borderline to describe the fuzzy border of two psychiatric disorders. Those who are diagnosed with BPD are no longer identified on the spectrum of psychosis and neurosis.

Children with BPD are inconsistent in their feelings. They have difficulty identifying themselves and struggle to maintain relationships. Children with BPD are often afraid of being abandoned. Emotionally they feel like they are on a roller coaster ride: they feel out of control and in a state where their emotions are constantly going up and down.

Although accurate information is readily available, unfortunately, we are still surrounded by lots of misinformation. This makes it difficult to separate what is authentic from what is just fiction. This phenomenon makes recovery much more difficult.

Studies have found a 10-20 percent chance that a first-degree relative will have BPD if you have BPD. This is relatively low, but you still have to factor in the 1.6 percent chance of the prevalence rate of BPD. This puts you at risk of getting BPD if your relative has already been diagnosed with BPD, which is 12 times higher than the general population.

Symptoms of BPD are very distressing. Children and adults diagnosed with BPD often feel like there life is out of control. Having overwhelming emotions makes their life miserable, and going through it every day becomes a struggle. Unfortunately, many children and adults with BPD have to live with this disorder and other psychiatric disorders that tend to go along with BPD.

Psychological treatments involve meeting a mental health professional regularly and explaining the struggles your child has to go through daily.

These professionals will help identify the root of problems and give advice on how to address the issues.

Medication treatment involves meeting a psychiatrist, getting an evaluation on the medication that may work in your child's case, and receiving a prescription. The meeting with psychiatrists has to be held regularly to evaluate the progress and look out for any side effects of the medicine your child is consuming.

Resources

[1] Gunderson, J. G., Herpertz, S. C., Skodol, A. E., Torgersen, S., & Zanarini, M. C. (2018). Borderline personality disorder. *Nature Reviews Disease Primers*, 4(1), 1-20.

[1] Fonagy, P., & Luyten, P. (2016). A multilevel perspective on the development of borderline personality disorder.

[1] Chanen, A. M. (2015). Borderline personality disorder in young people: are we there yet?. *Journal of Clinical Psychology*, 71(8), 778-791.

[1] Biskin, R. S. (2015). The lifetime course of borderline personality disorder. *The Canadian Journal of Psychiatry*, 60(7), 303-308.

[1] Biskin, R. S. (2015). The lifetime course of borderline personality disorder. *The Canadian Journal of Psychiatry*, 60(7), 303-308.

[1] MacIntosh, H. B., Godbout, N., & Dubash, N. (2015). Borderline personality disorder: Disorder of trauma or

personality, a review of the empirical literature. *Canadian Psychology/Psychologie Canadienne, 56*(2), 227.

[1] Miano, A., Grosselli, L., Roepke, S., & Dziobek, I. (2017). Emotional dysregulation in borderline personality disorder and its influence on communication behavior and feelings in romantic relationships. *Behaviour research and therapy, 95*, 148-157.

[1] Euler, S., Nolte, T., Constantinou, M., Griem, J., Montague, P. R., Fonagy, P., & Personality and Mood Disorders Research Network. (2021). Interpersonal problems in borderline personality disorder: associations with mentalizing, emotion regulation, and impulsiveness. *Journal of personality disorders, 35*(2), 177-193.

[1] Chapman, A. L. (2019). Borderline personality disorder and emotion dysregulation. *Development and Psychopathology, 31*(3), 1143-1156.

[1] Tucker, R. P., Lengel, G. J., Smith, C. E., Capron, D. W., Mullins-Sweatt, S. N., & Wingate, L. R. (2016). Maladaptive five factor model personality traits associated with borderline personality disorder indirectly affect susceptibility to suicide

ideation through increased anxiety sensitivity cognitive concerns. *Psychiatry research, 246,* 432-437.

[1] Brand, B. L., Sar, V., Stavropoulos, P., Krüger, C., Korzekwa, M., Martínez-Taboas, A., & Middleton, W. (2016). Separating fact from fiction: An empirical examination of six myths about dissociative identity disorder. *Harvard review of psychiatry.*

[1] Kuczynski, J. M. (2020). The Myth of Borderline Personality Disorder.

[1] Temes, C. M., Frankenburg, F. R., Fitzmaurice, G. M., & Zanarini, M. C. (2019). Deaths by suicide and other causes among patients with borderline personality disorder and personality-disordered comparison subjects over 24 years of prospective follow-up. *The Journal of clinical psychiatry, 80*(1), 0-0.

[1] Temes, C. M., & Zanarini, M. C. (2018). The longitudinal course of borderline personality disorder. *Psychiatric Clinics, 41*(4), 685-694.

[1] Sauer-Zavala, S., Bentley, K. H., & Wilner, J. G. (2016). Transdiagnostic treatment of borderline personality disorder

and comorbid disorders: A clinical replication series. *Journal of personality disorders*, *30*(1), 35-51.

[1] Biskin, R. S. (2015). The lifetime course of borderline personality disorder. *The Canadian Journal of Psychiatry*, *60*(7), 303-308.

[1] Fineberg, S. K., Gupta, S., & Leavitt, J. (2019). Collaborative deprescribing in borderline personality disorder: A narrative review. *Harvard review of psychiatry*, *27*(2), 75-86.

[1] Choi-Kain, L. W., Finch, E. F., Masland, S. R., Jenkins, J. A., & Unruh, B. T. (2017). What works in the treatment of borderline personality disorder. *Current behavioral neuroscience reports*, *4*(1), 21-30.

[1] Chanen, A. M., Nicol, K., Betts, J. K., & Thompson, K. N. (2020). Diagnosis and treatment of borderline personality disorder in young people. *Current psychiatry reports*, *22*(5), 1-8.

[1] Knafo, A., Guilé, J. M., Breton, J. J., Labelle, R., Belloncle, V., Bodeau, N., ... & Gérardin, P. (2015). Coping strategies associated with suicidal behaviour in adolescent inpatients with borderline personality disorder. *Canadian journal of psychiatry. Revue canadienne de psychiatrie, 60*(2 Suppl 1), S46.

www.ingramcontent.com/pod-product-compliance
Lightning Source LLC
LaVergne TN
LVHW012108070526
838202LV00056B/5667